ALABRI Publications

Copyright © 2021

All rights reserced. No part of this publiction may be reproduced, distributed or transmitted in any form or by any means, including photocopying, recording or other electronic or mechanical methods without the prior written permission of the publisher, except in the case of brief quotations embodied in critical reviews and certain noncommercial uses permitted by copyright law.

DRAW AND WRITE

This Book

BELONGS TO

Draw

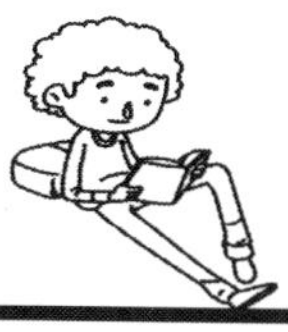

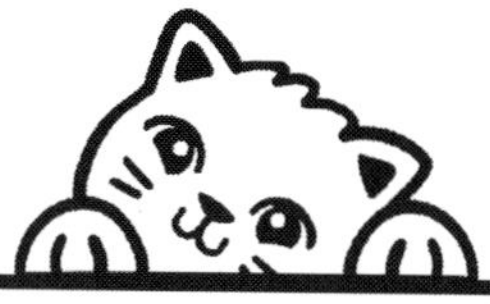

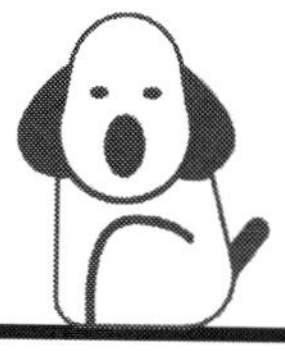

Write

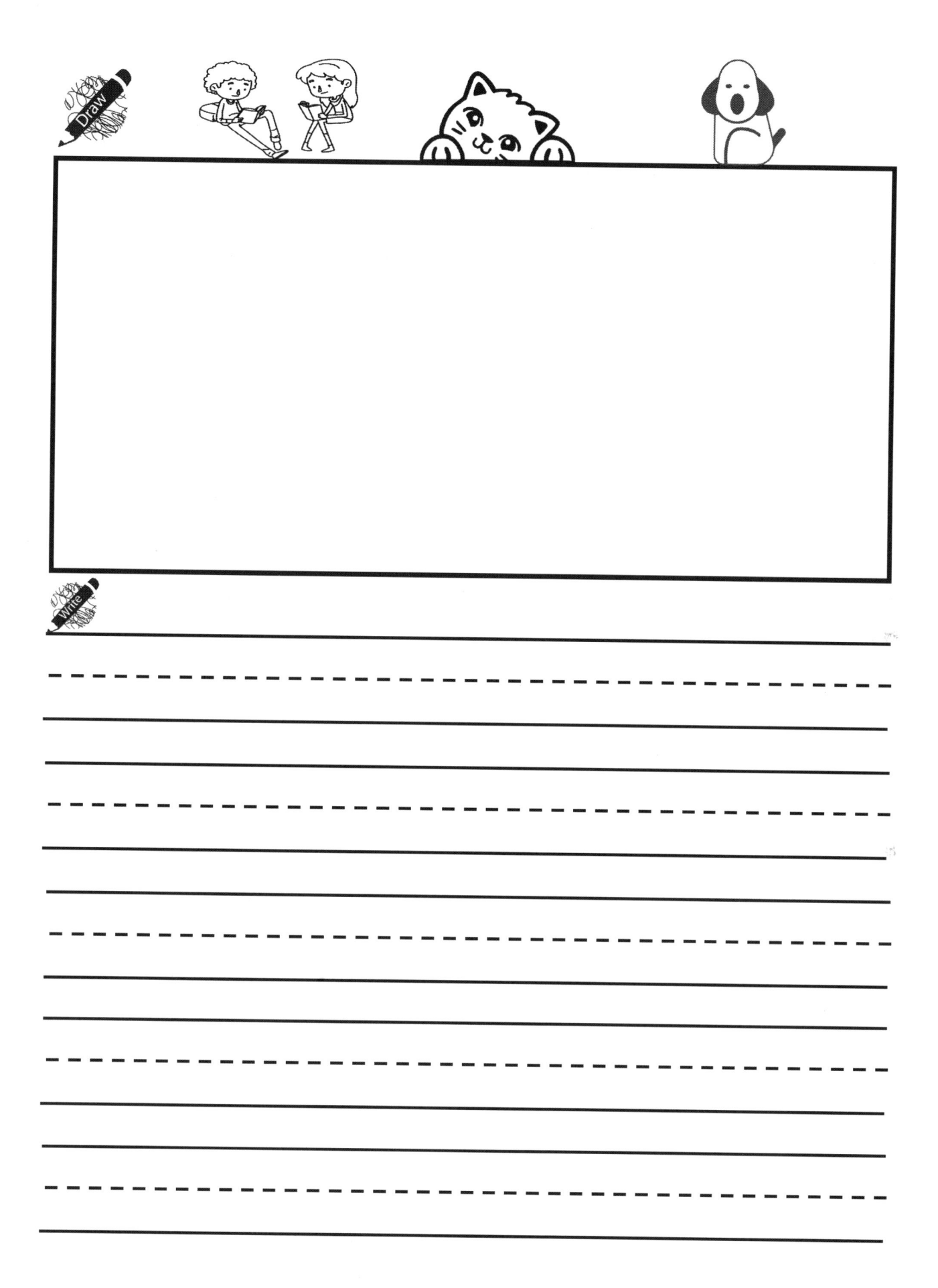

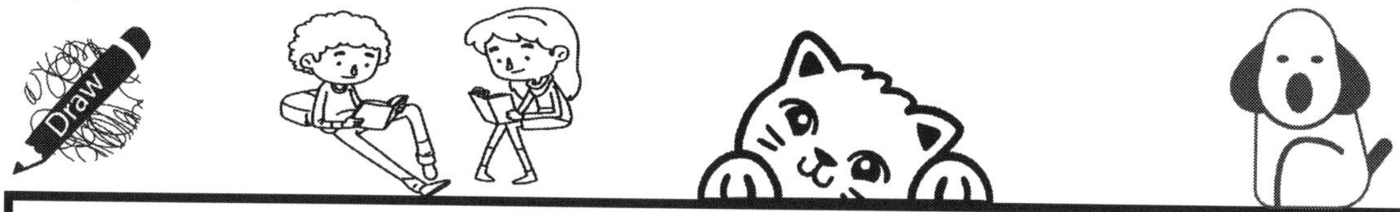

Write

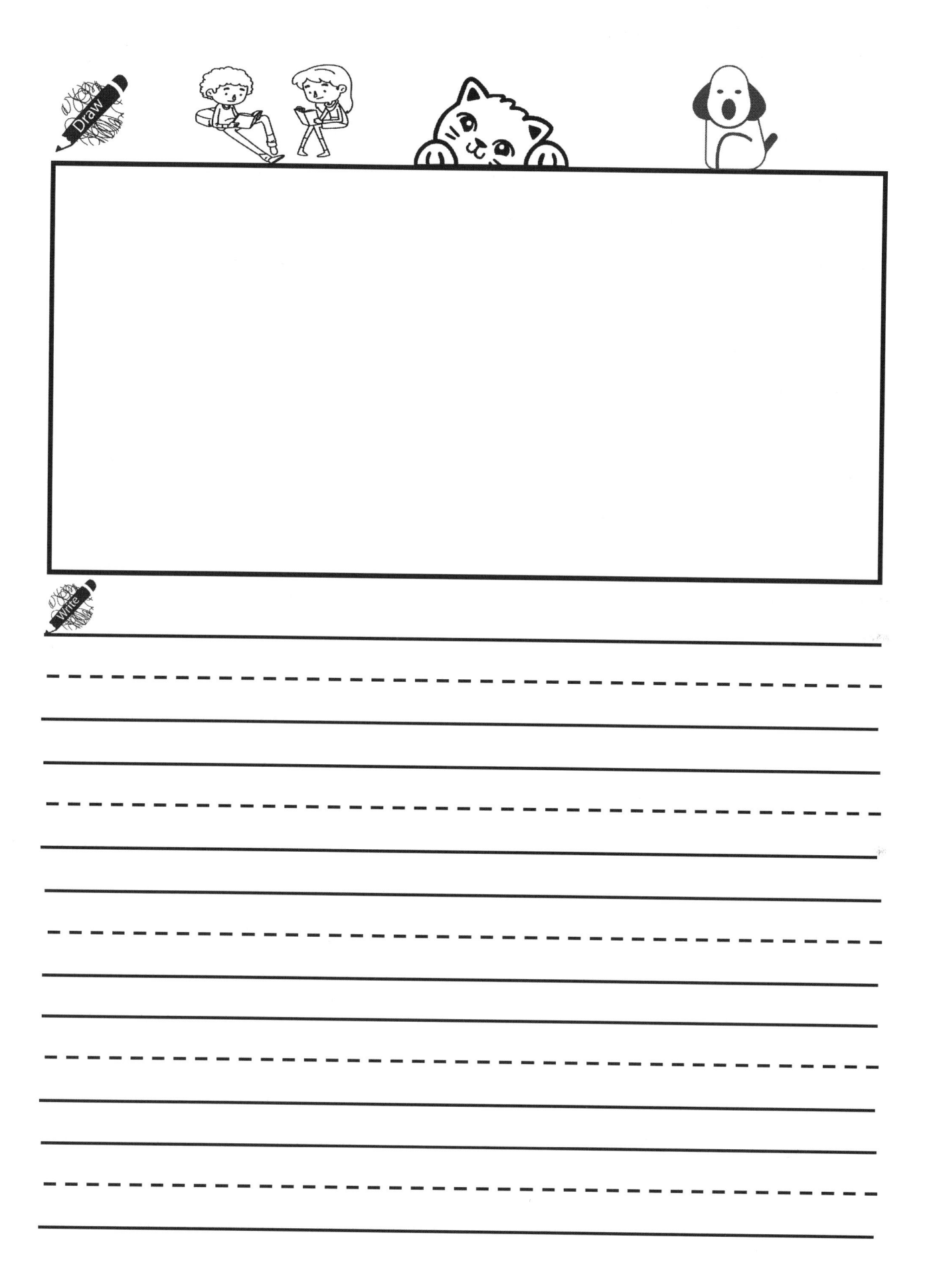

Draw

Write

Draw

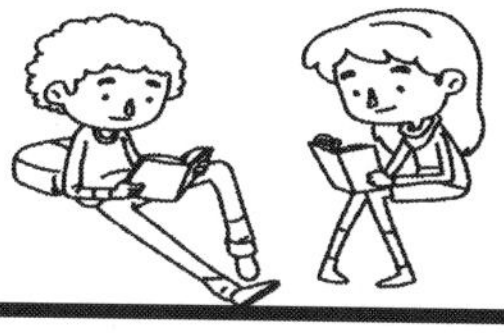

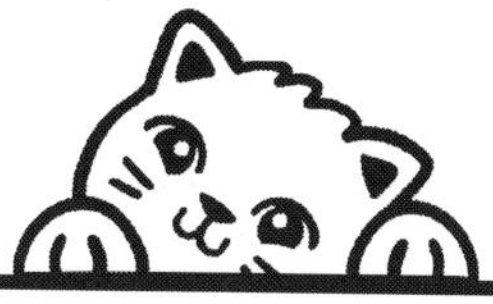

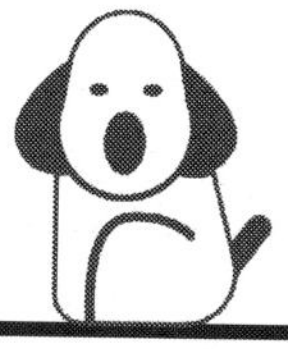

Write

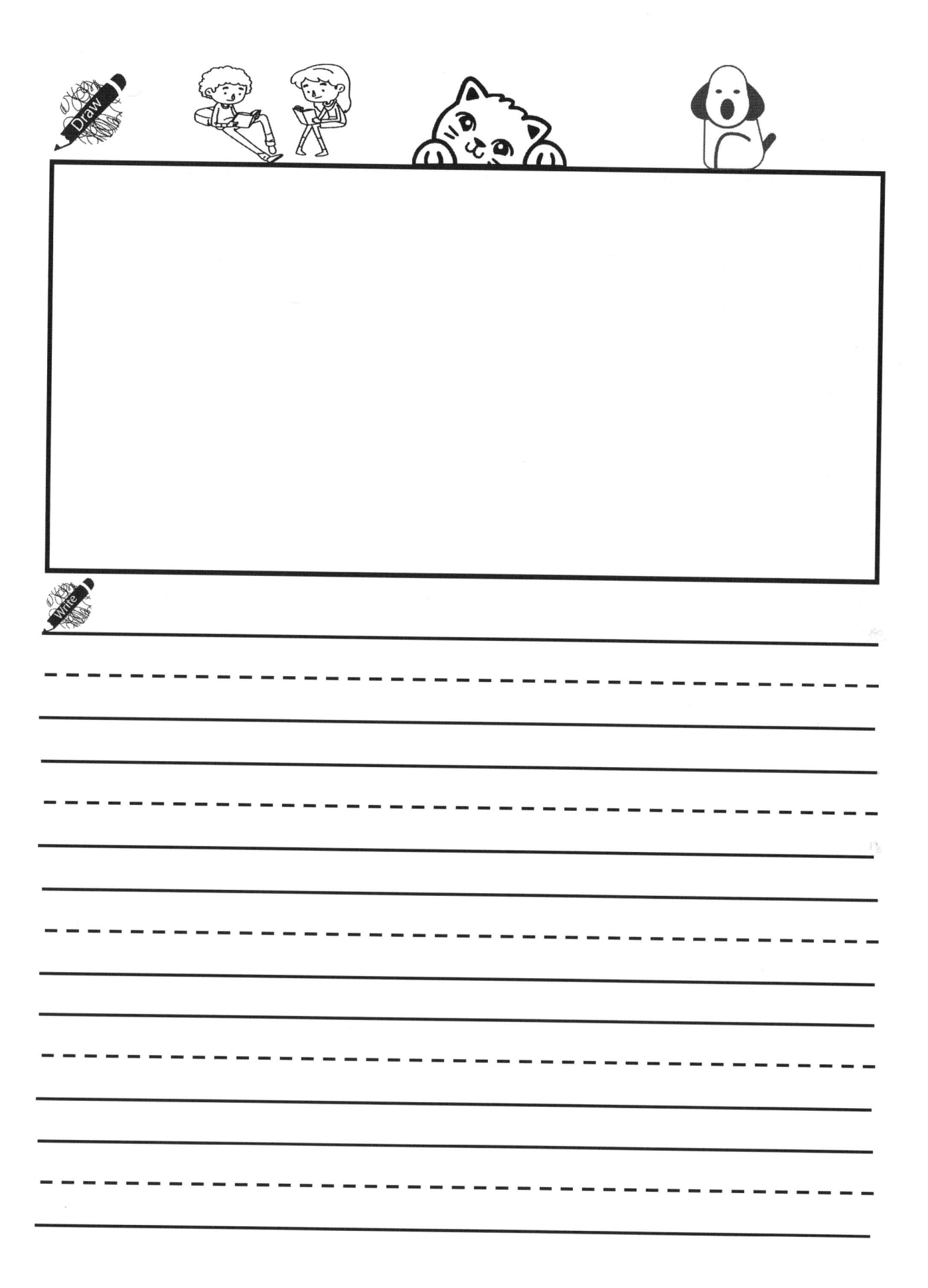

Draw

Write

Draw

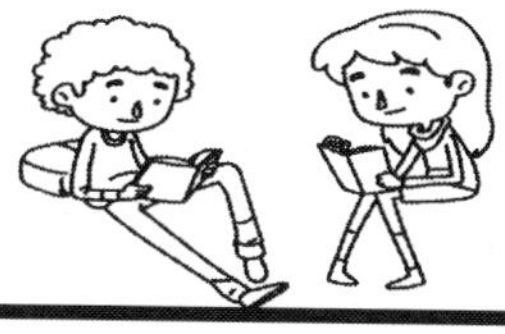

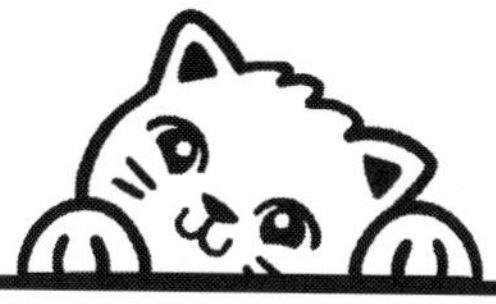

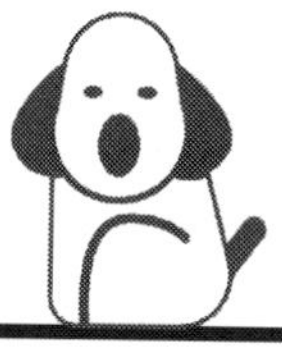

Write

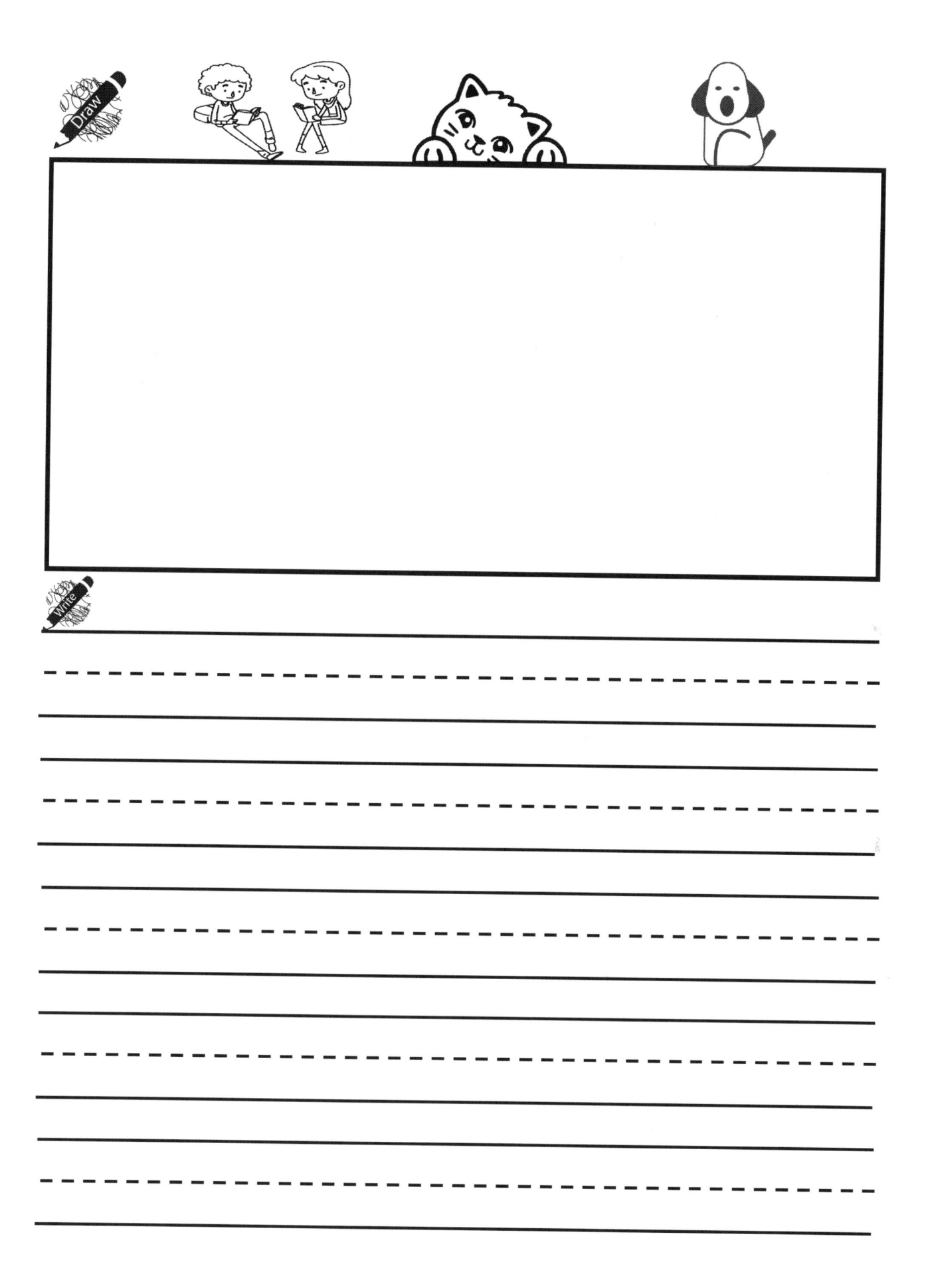

Draw

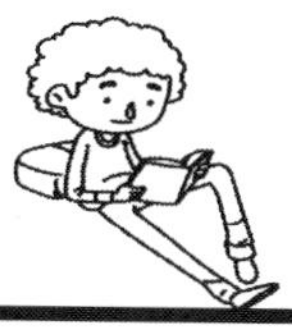

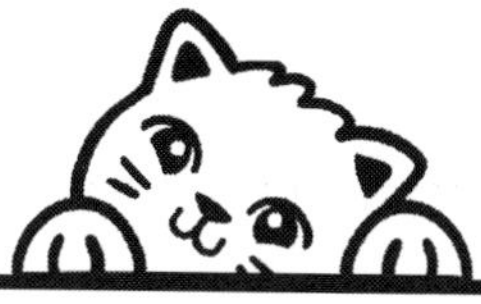

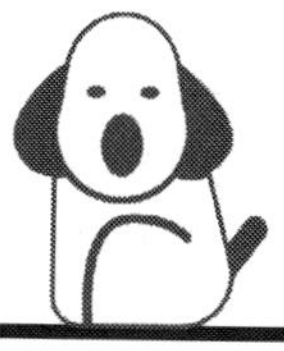

Write

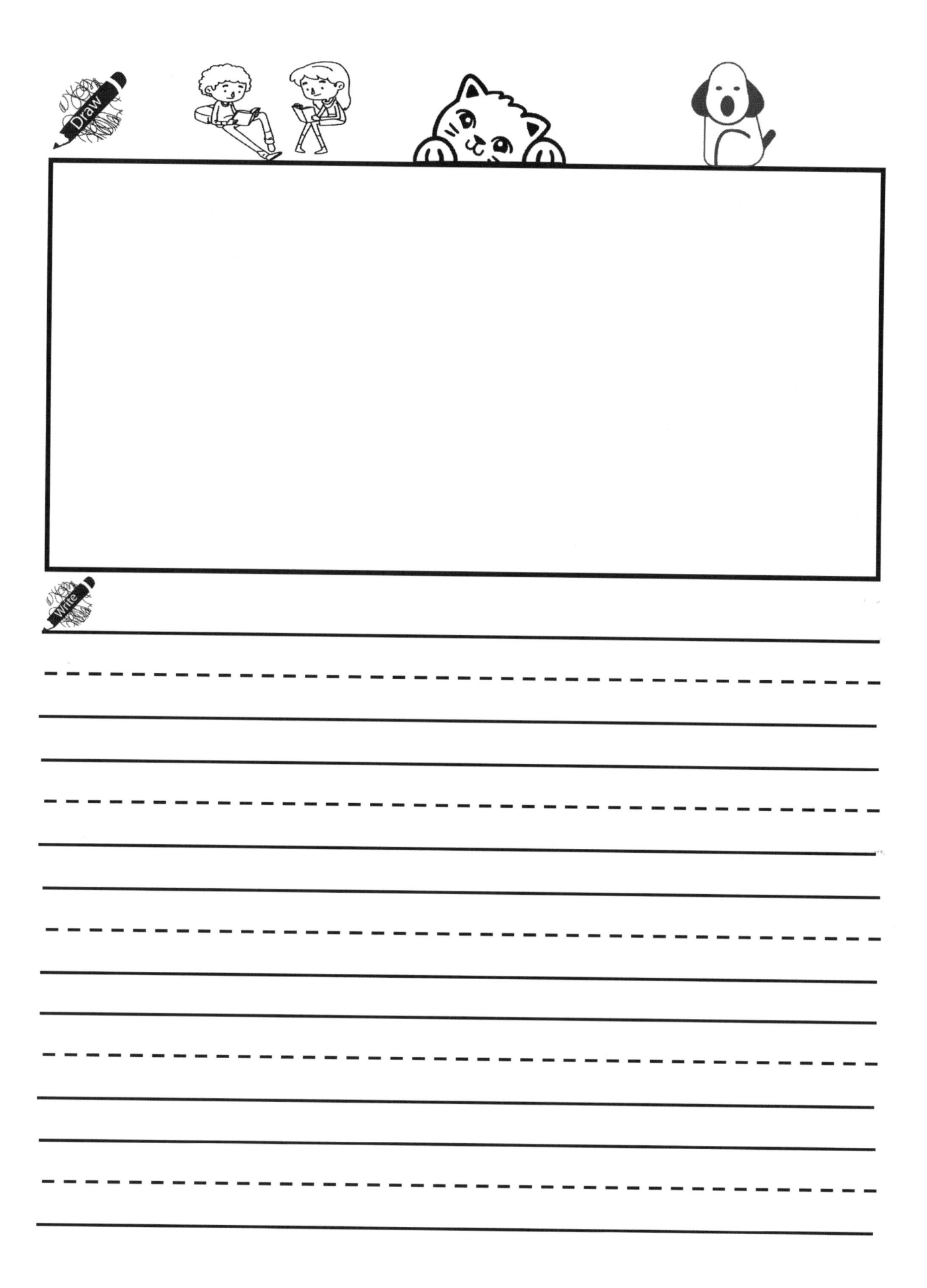

Draw

Write

Draw

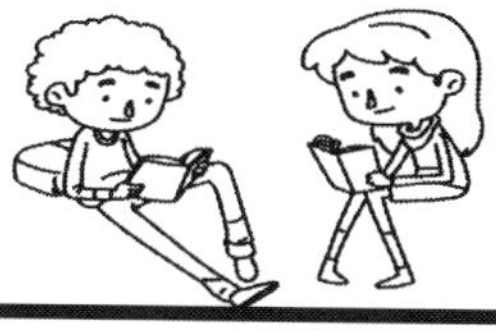

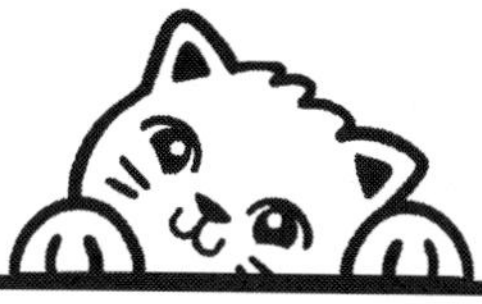

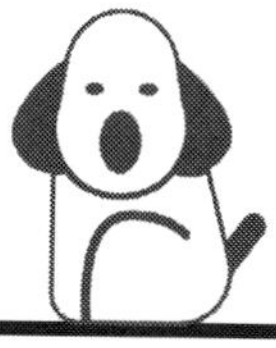

Write

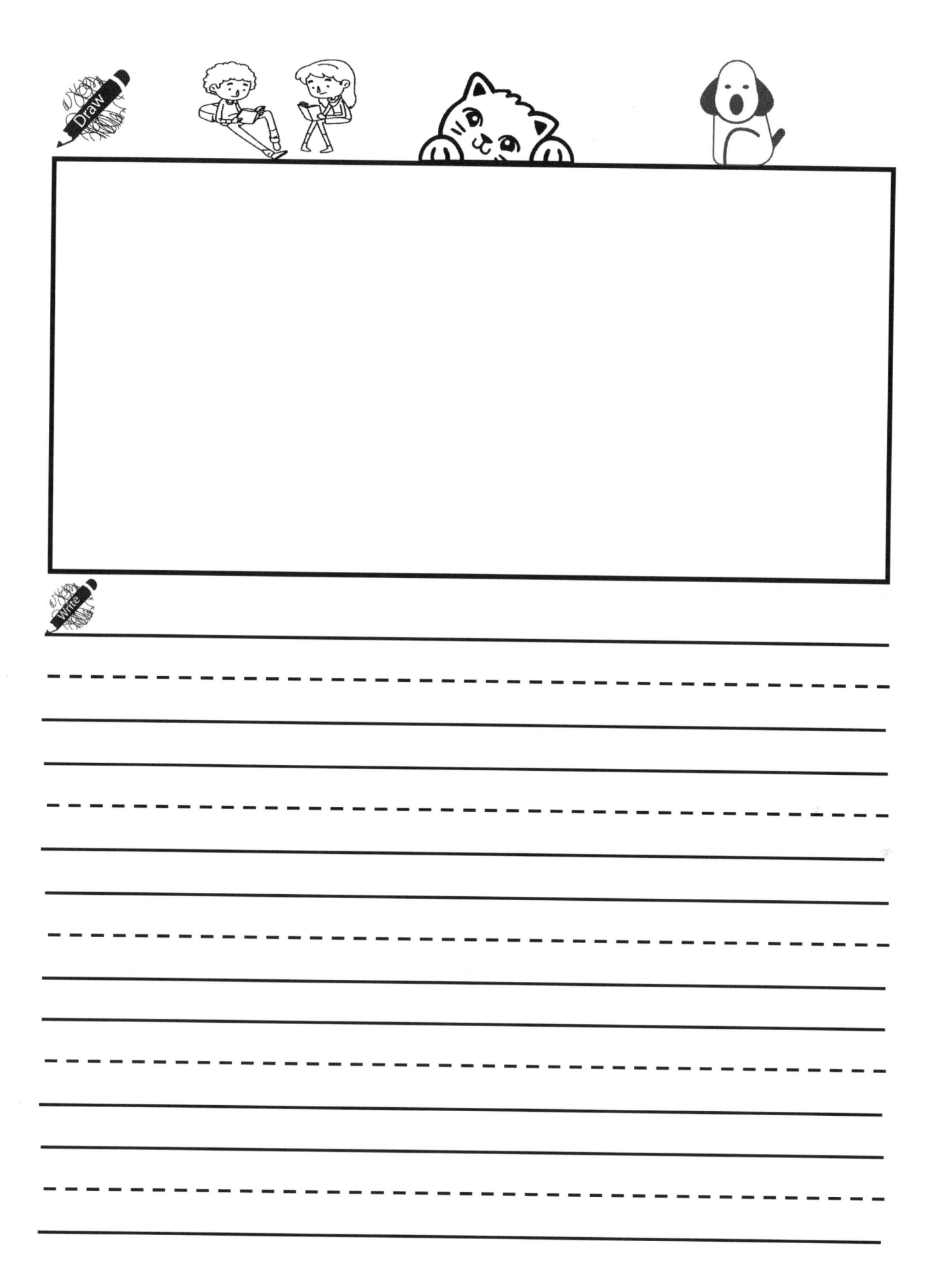

Draw

Write

Draw

Write

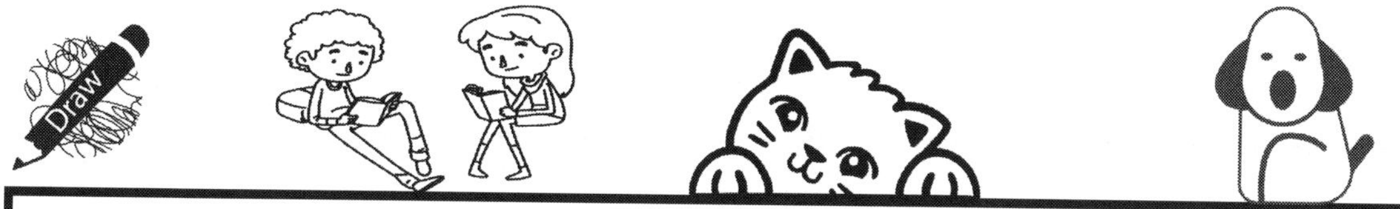

Write

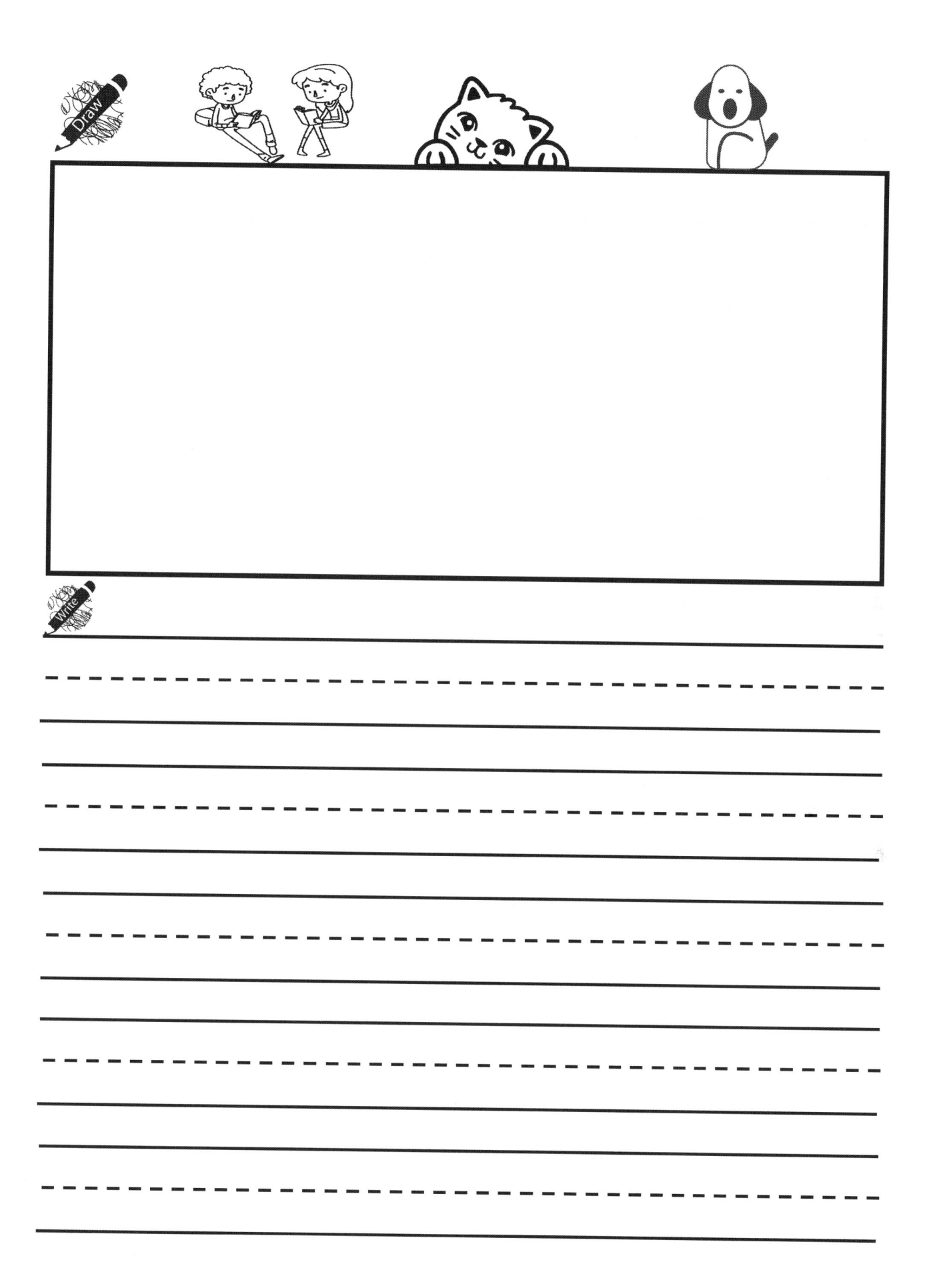

Draw

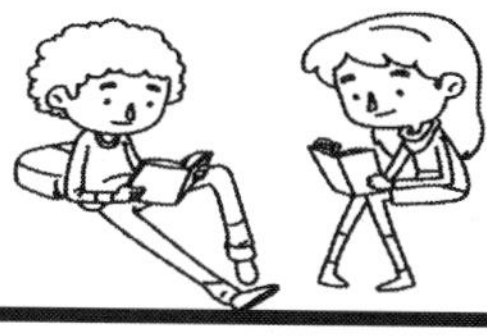

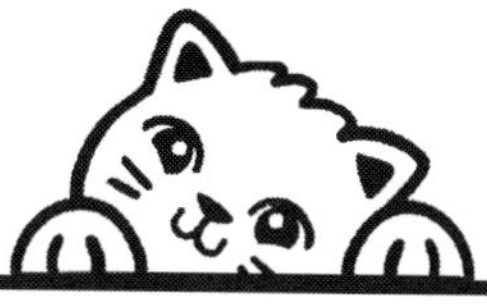

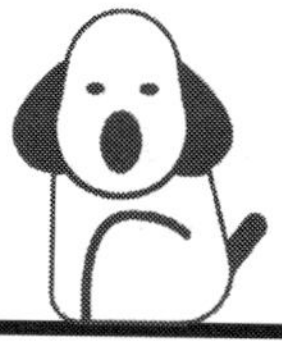

Write

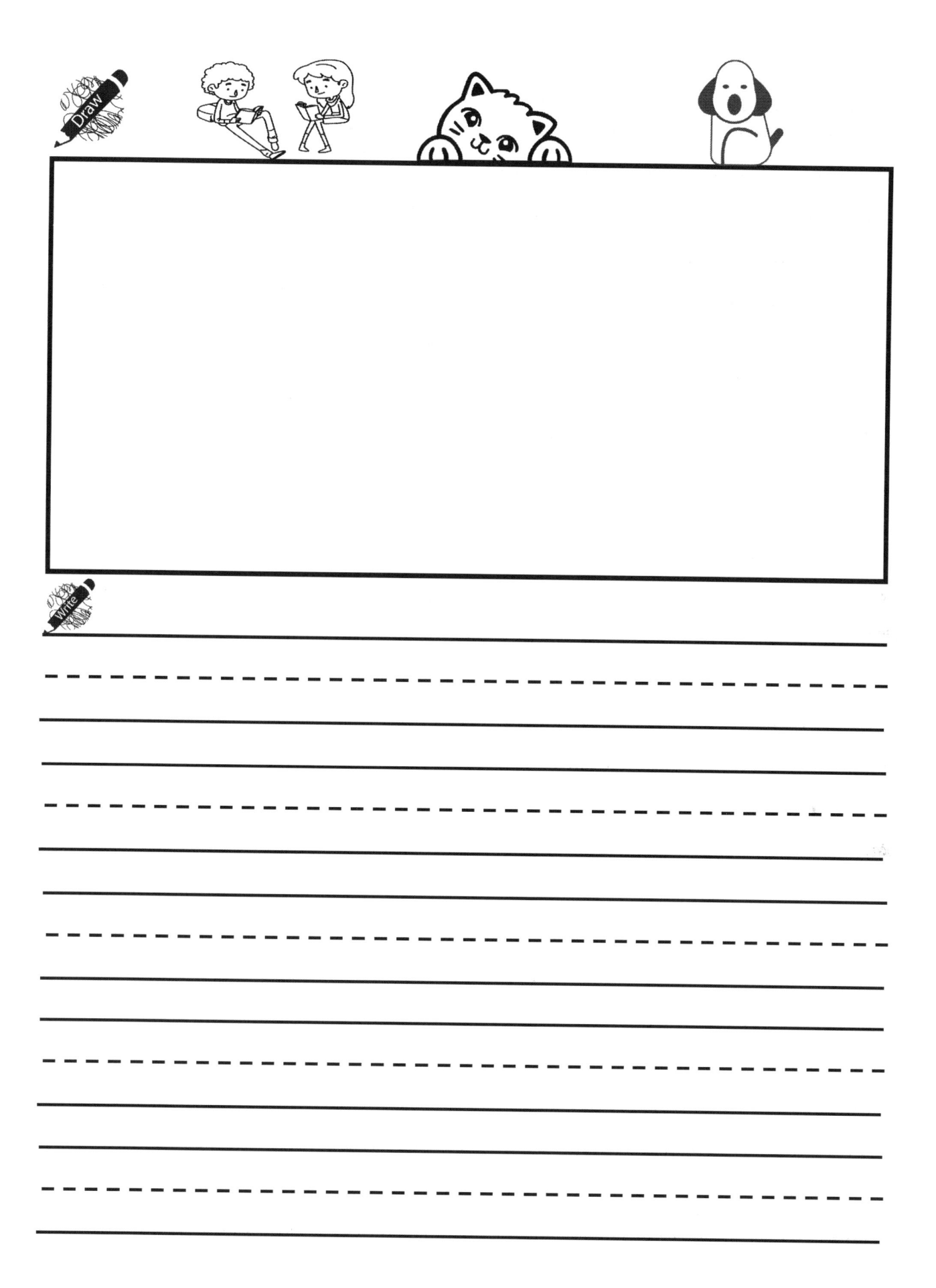

Draw

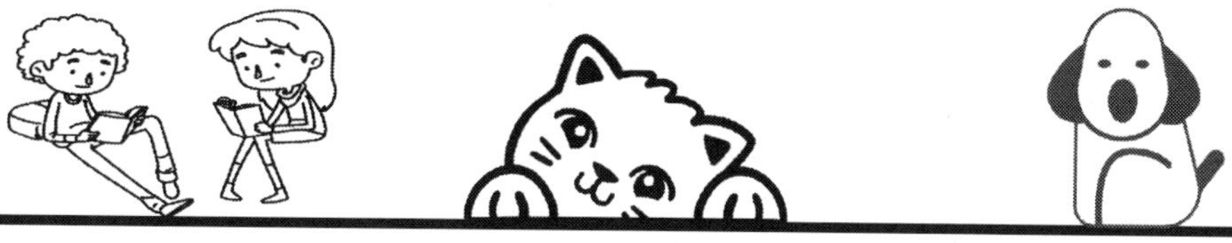

Write

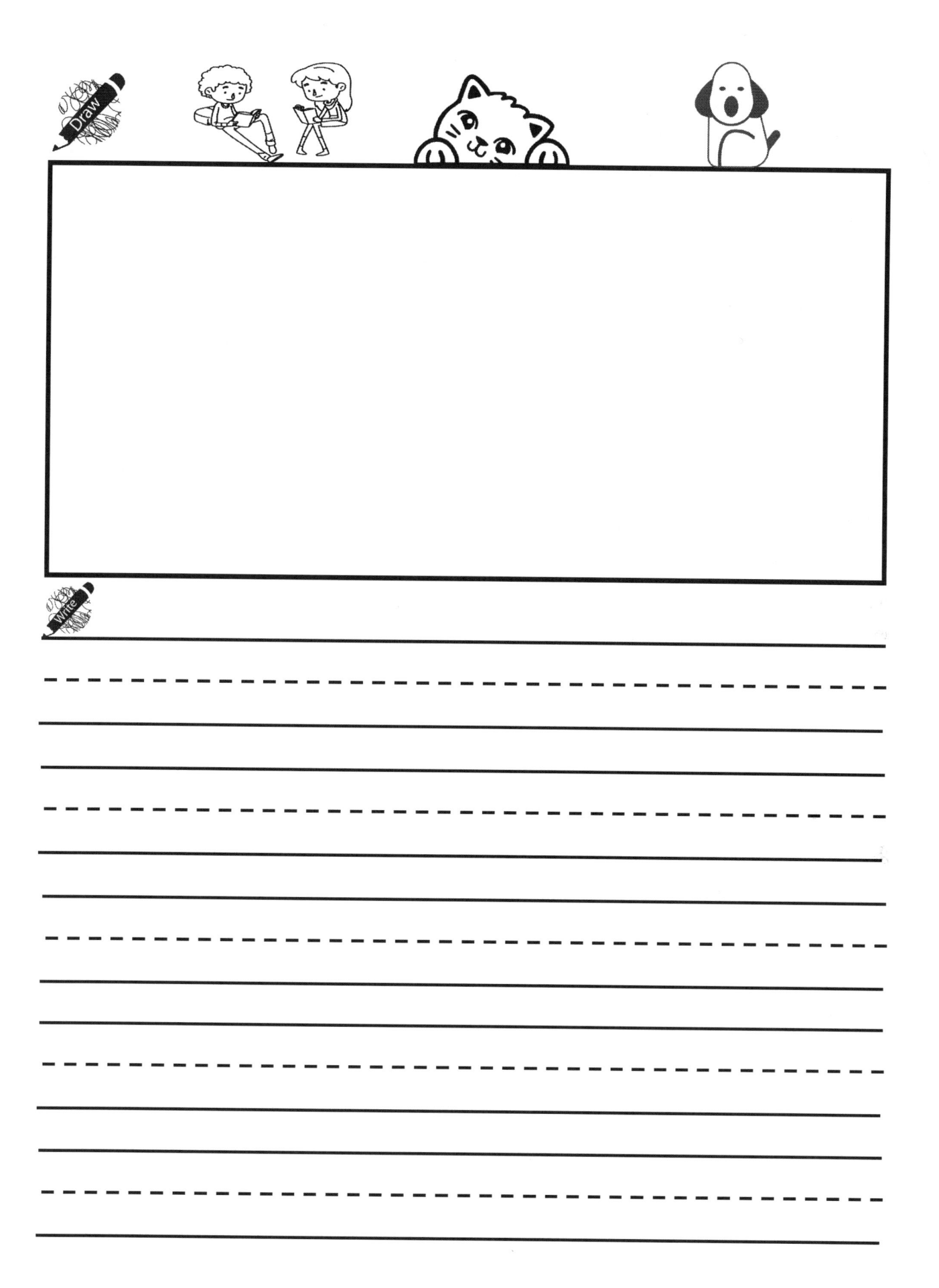

Draw

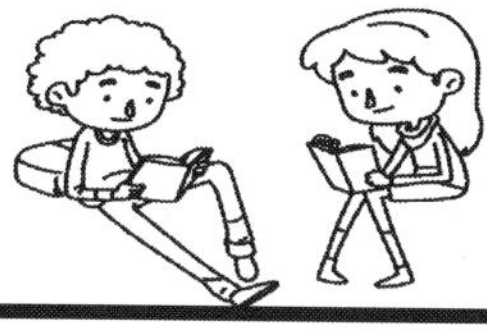

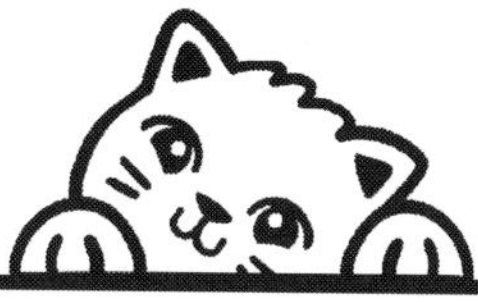

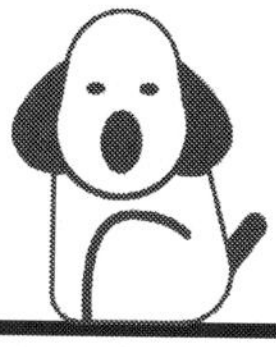

Write

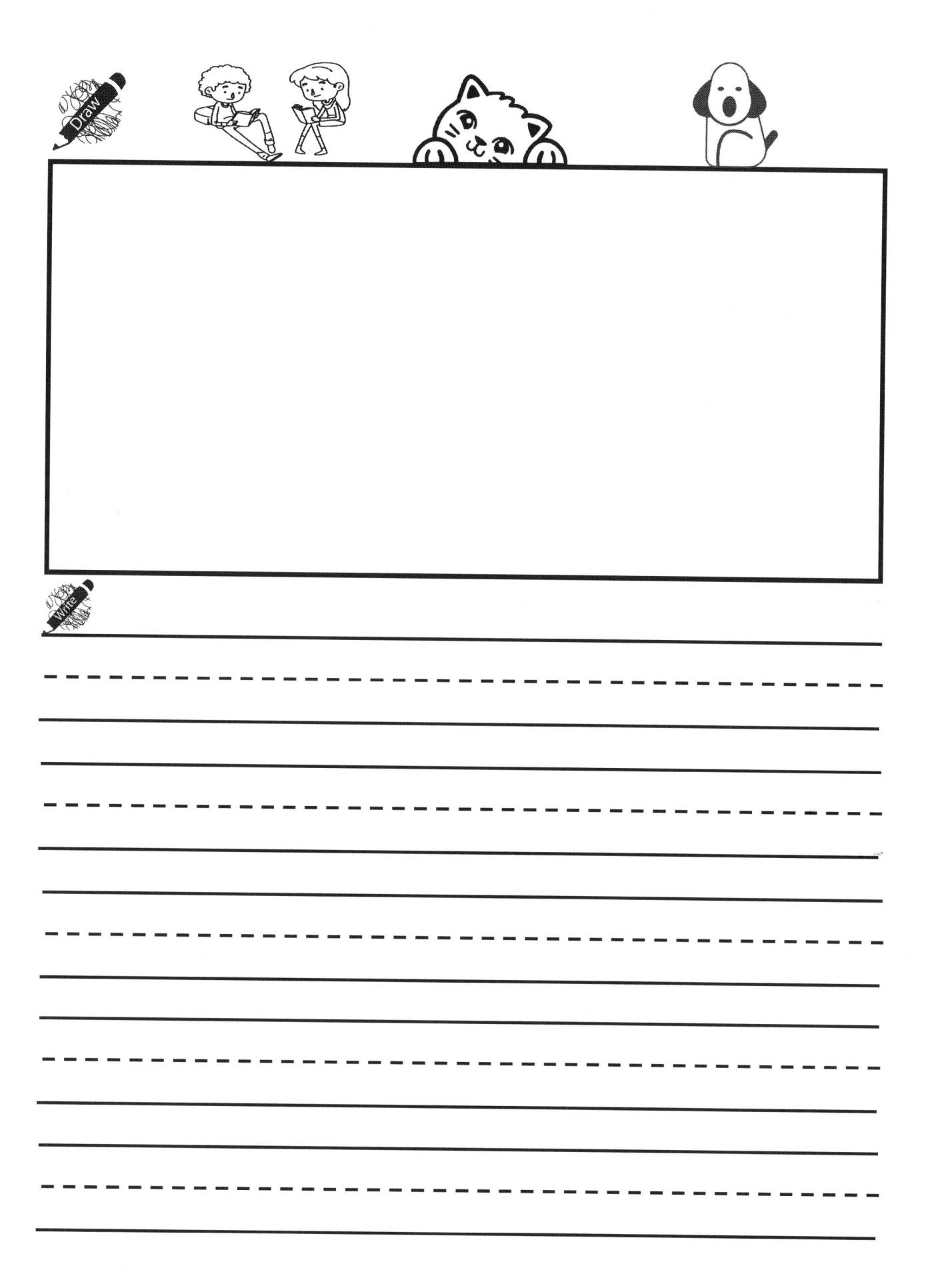

Draw

Write

Draw

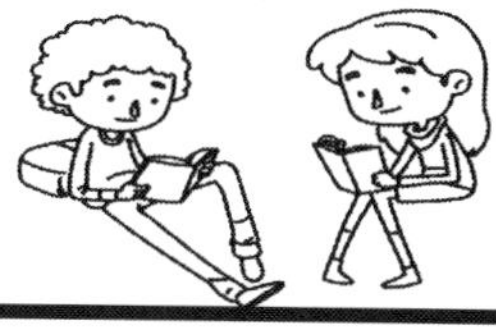

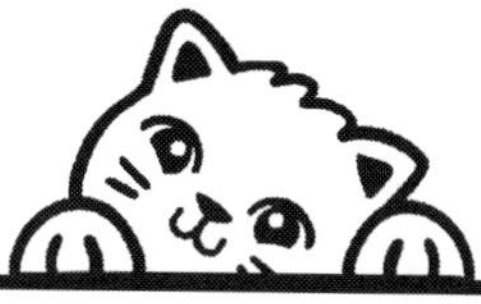

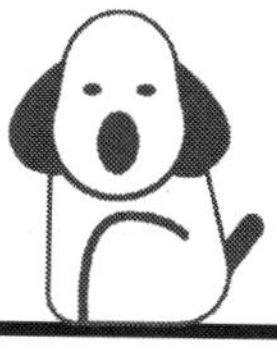

Write

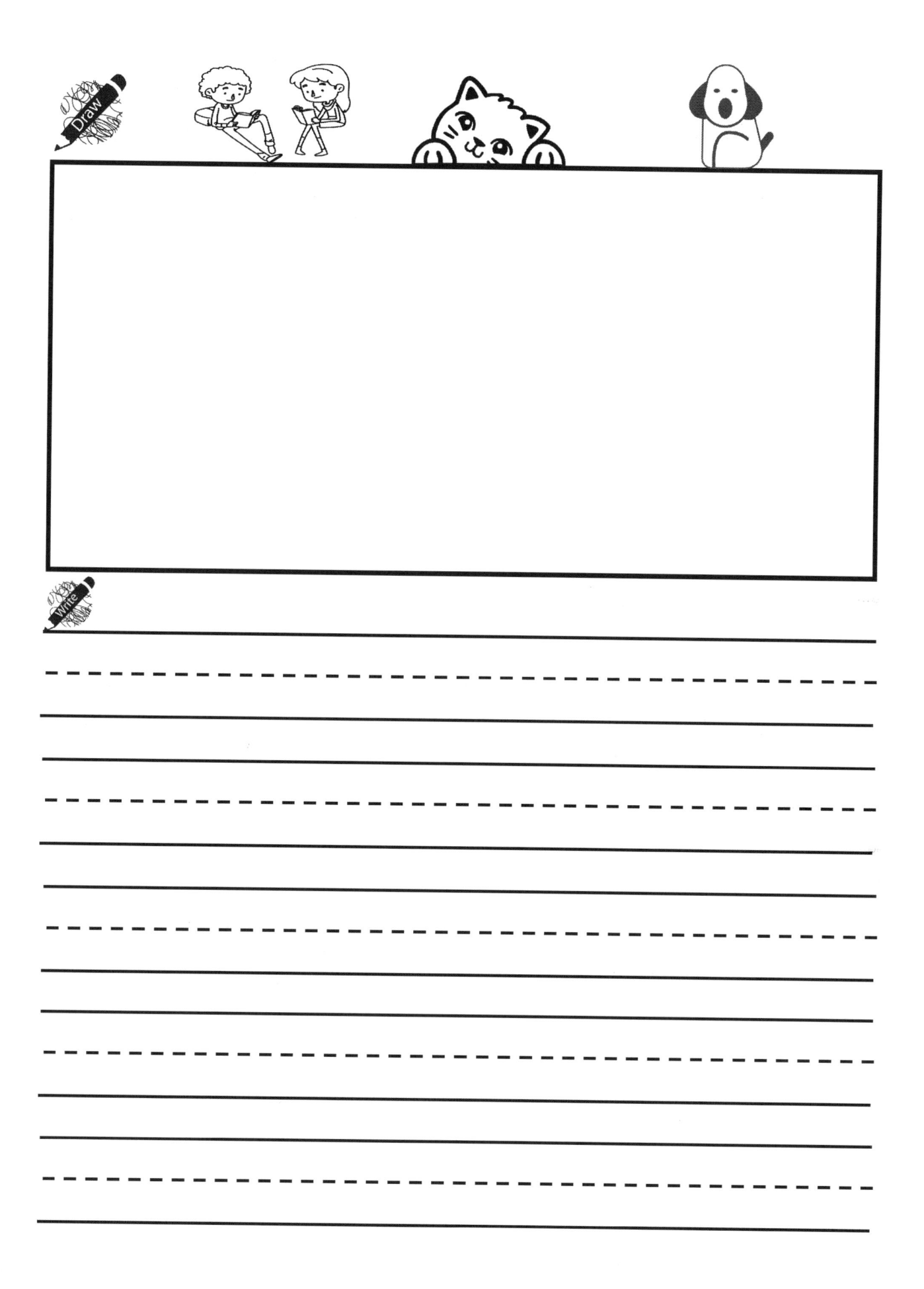

Draw

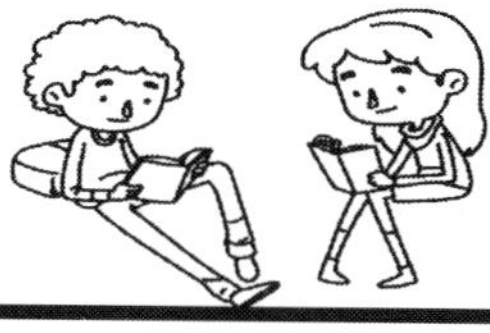

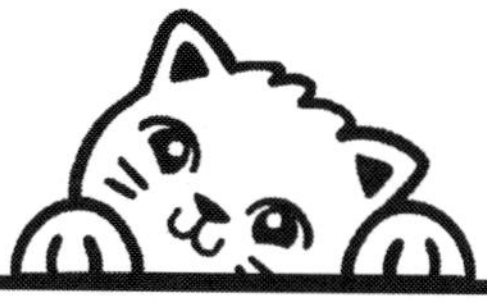

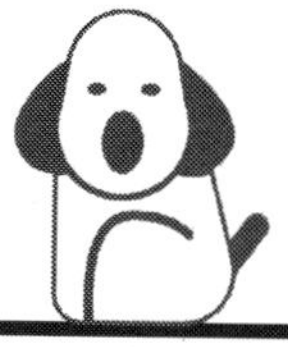

Write

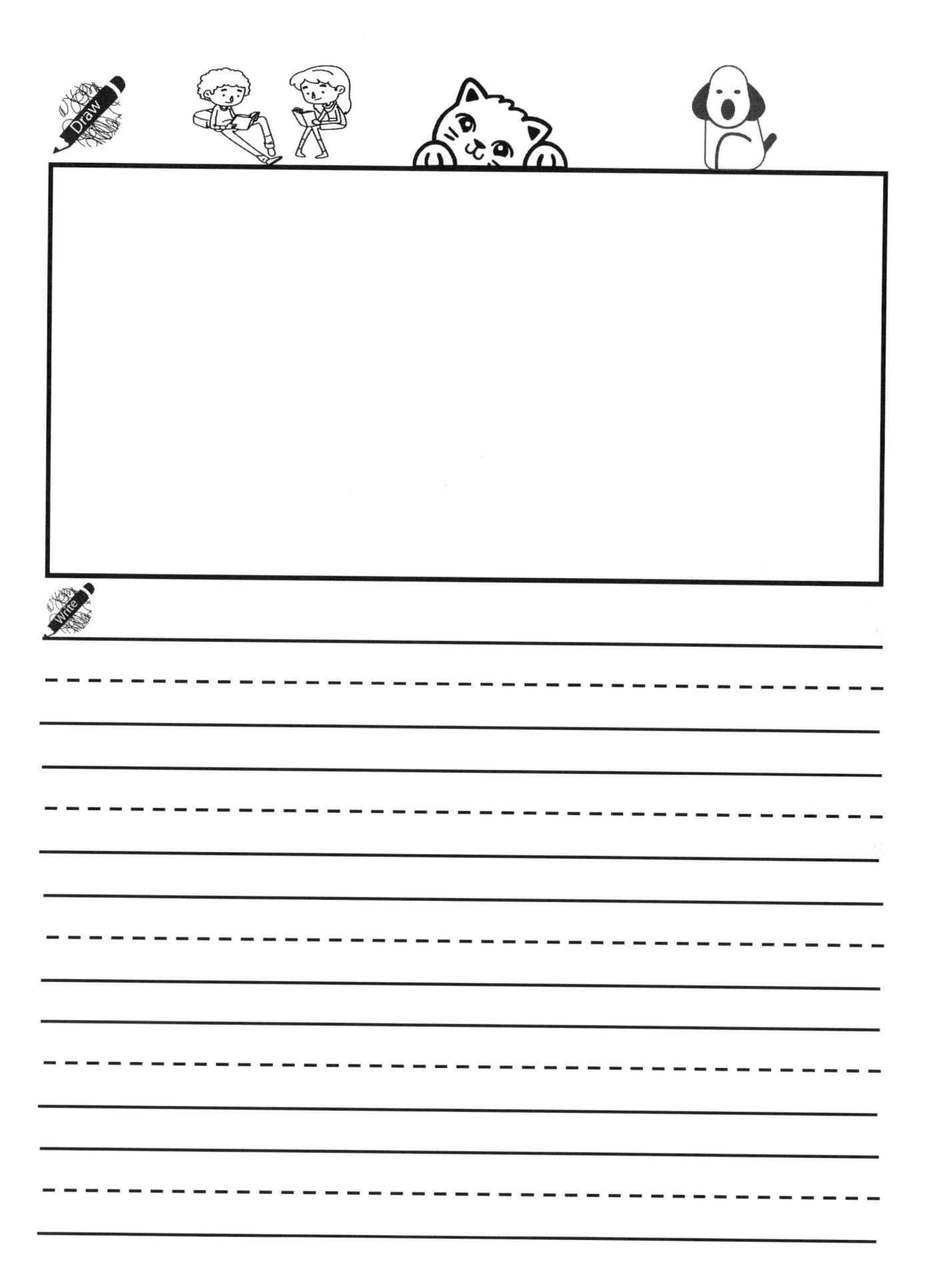

Draw

Write

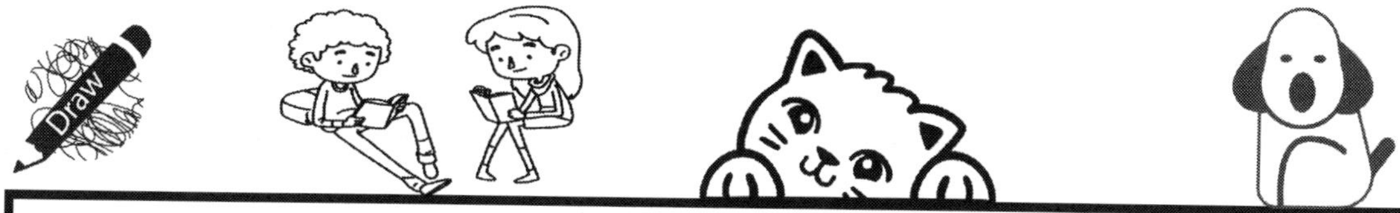
Draw

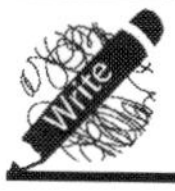
Write

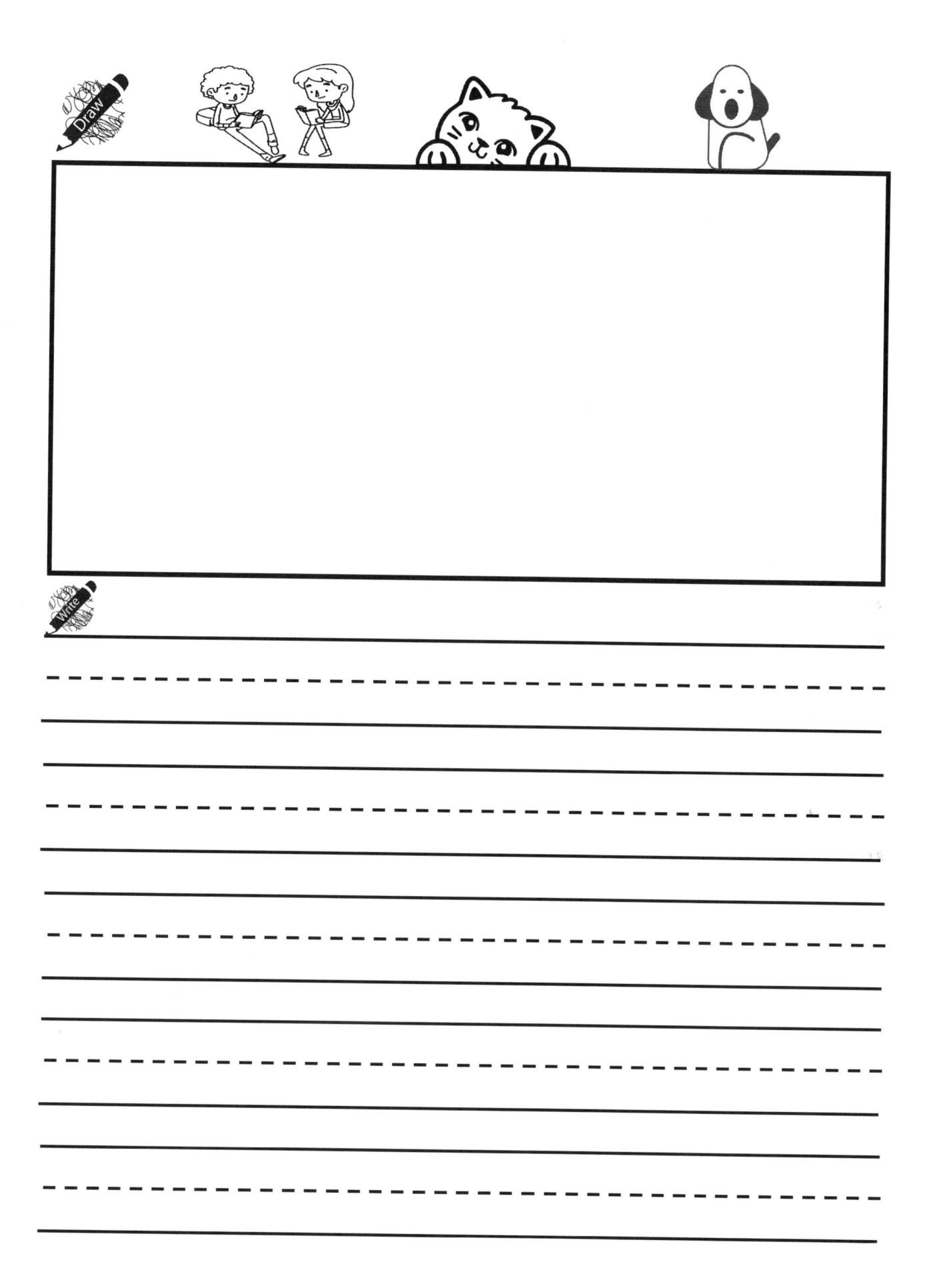

Draw

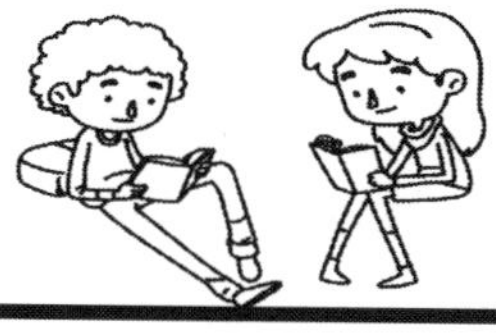

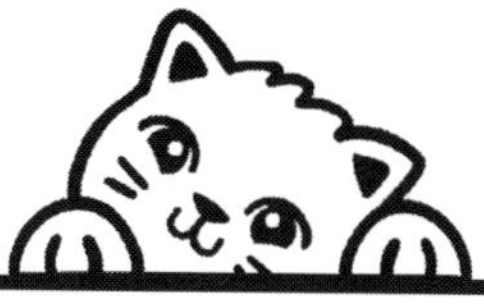

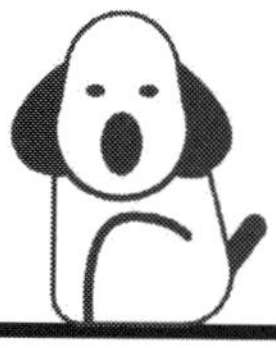

Write

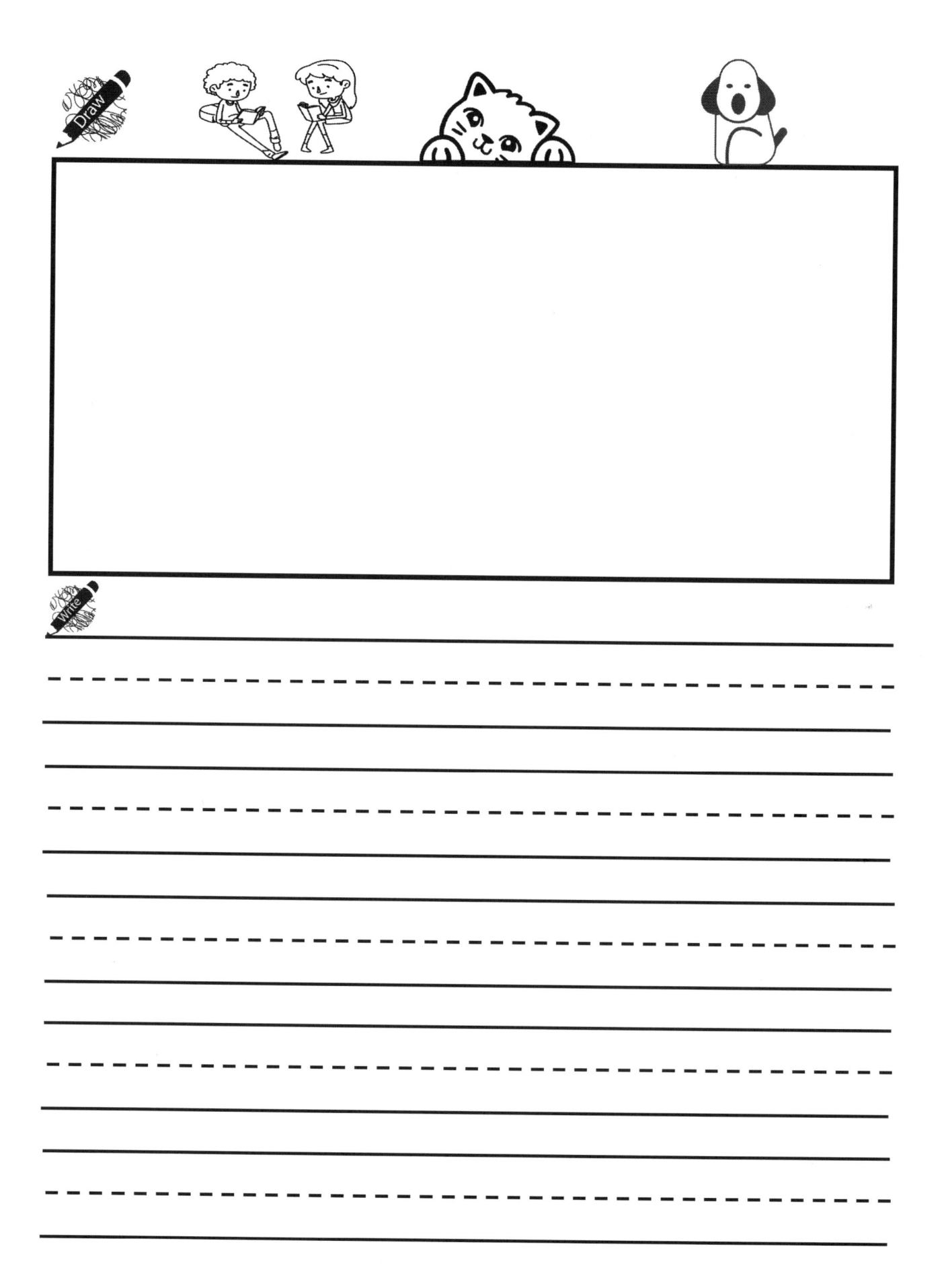

Draw

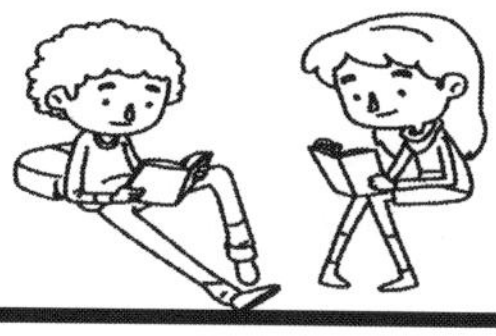

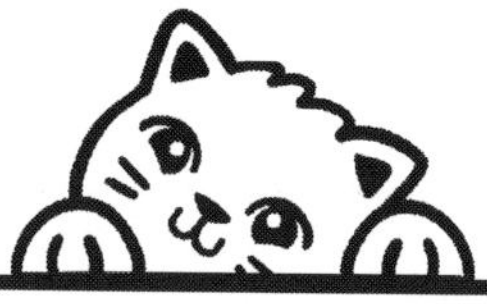

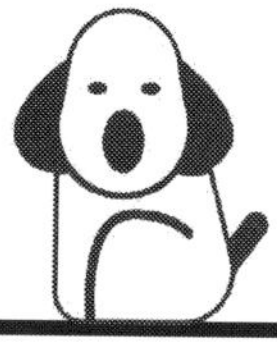

Write

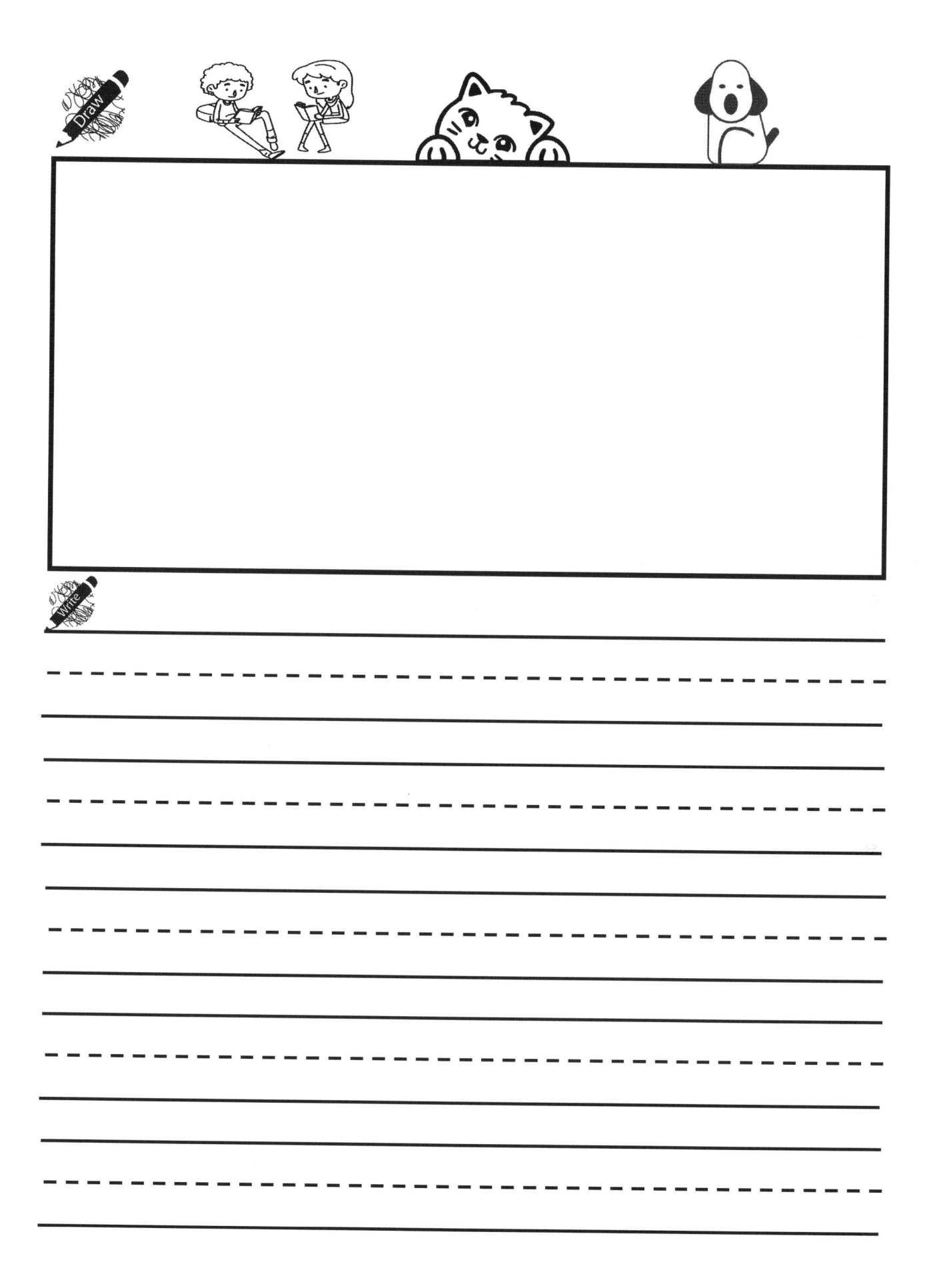

Draw

Write

Draw

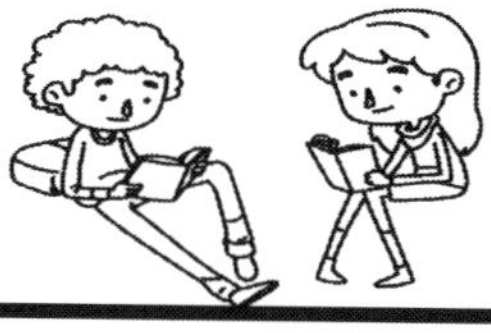

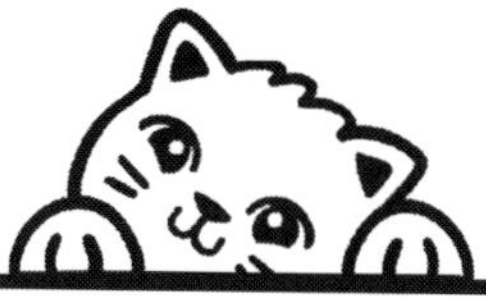

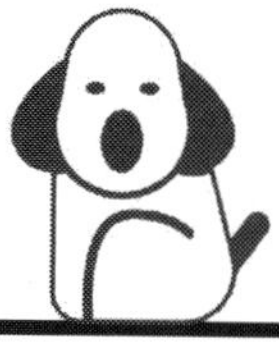

Write

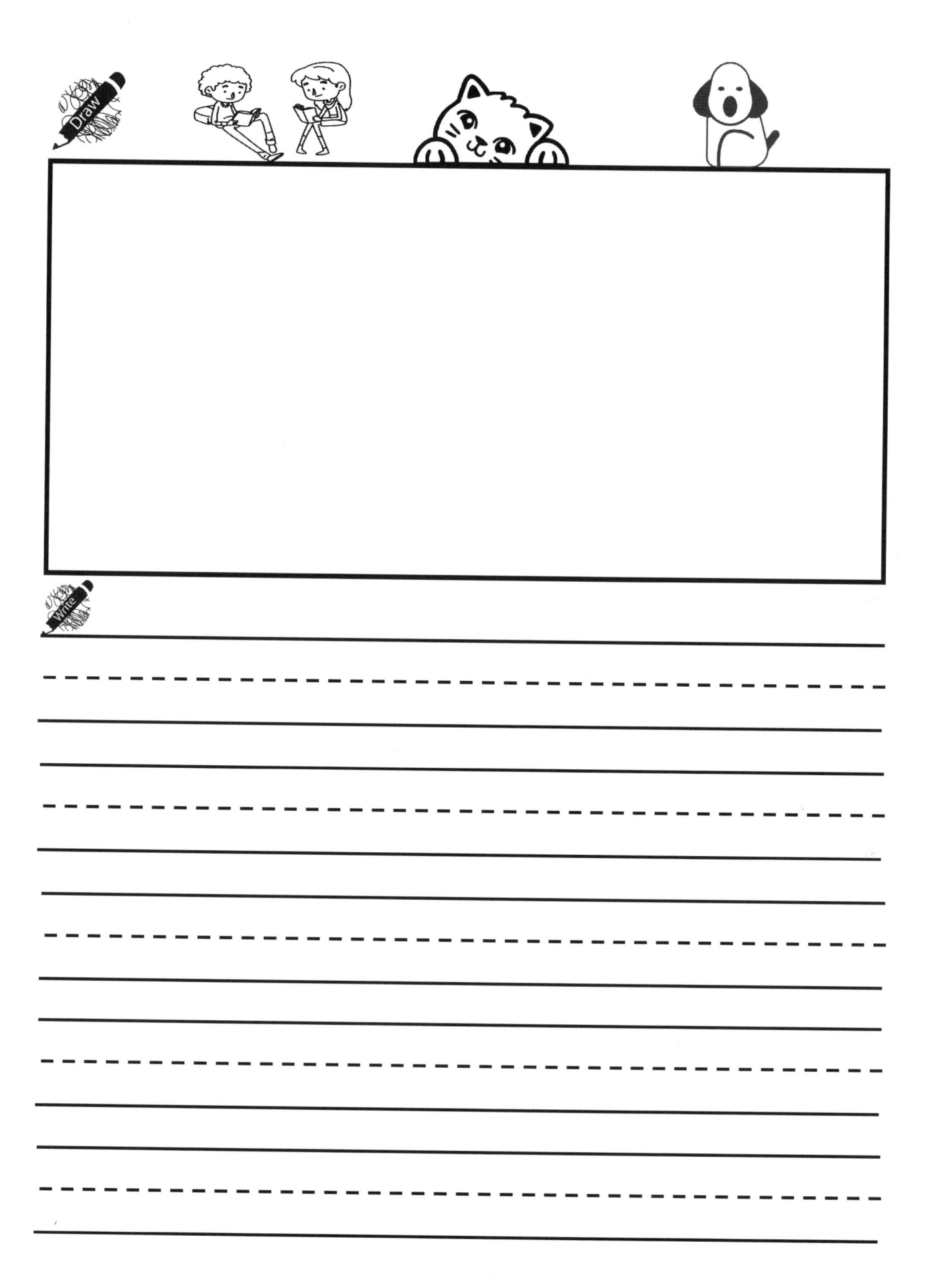

Draw

Write

Draw

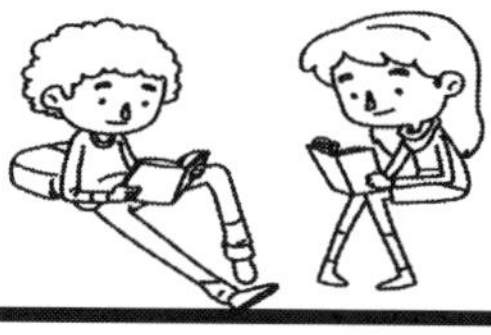

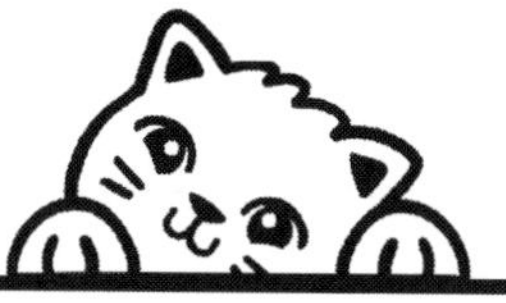

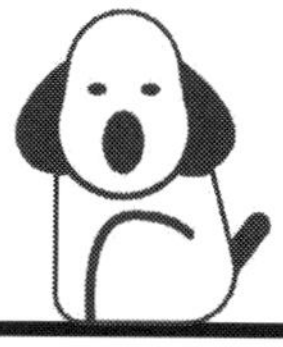

Write

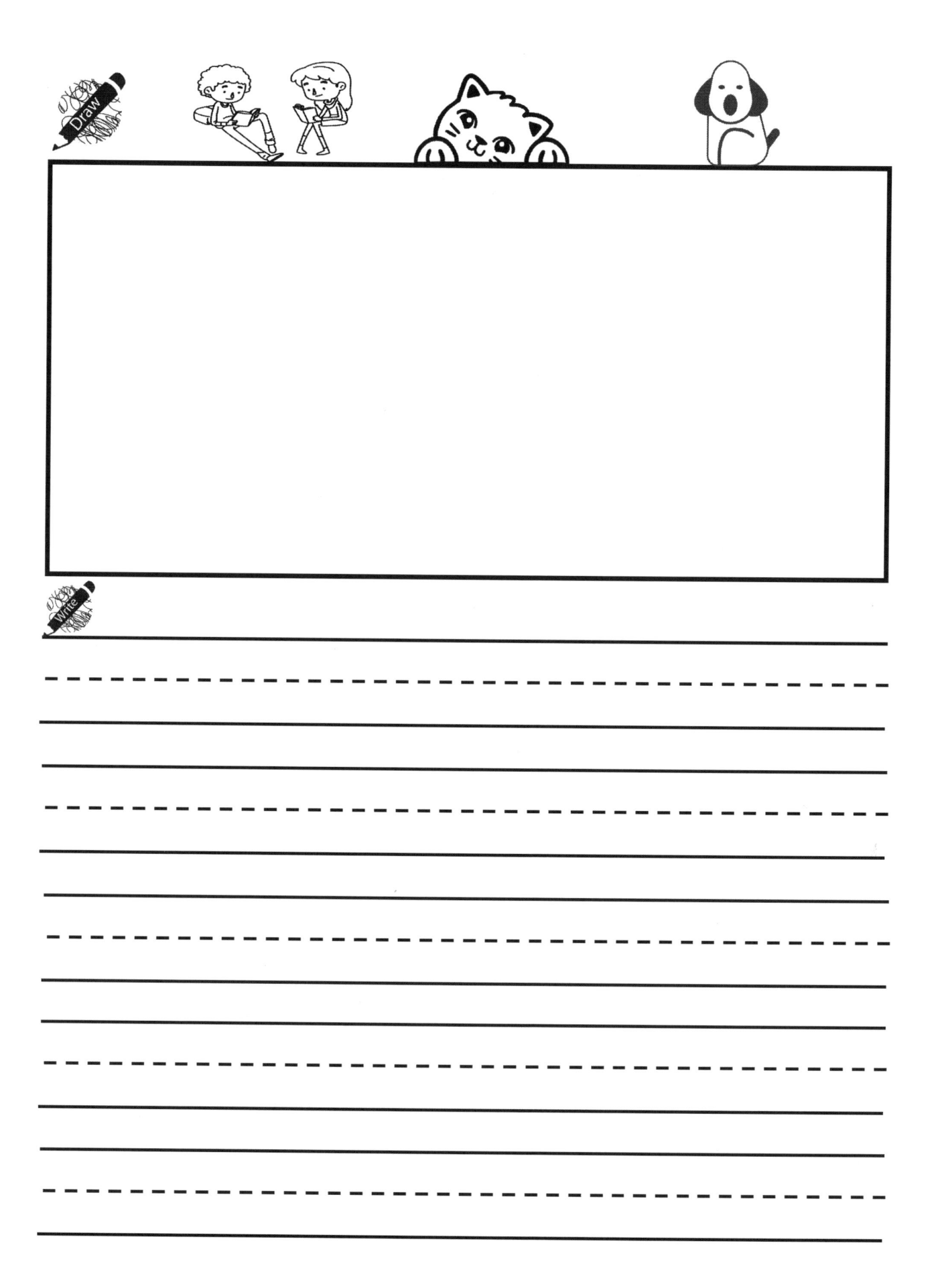

Draw

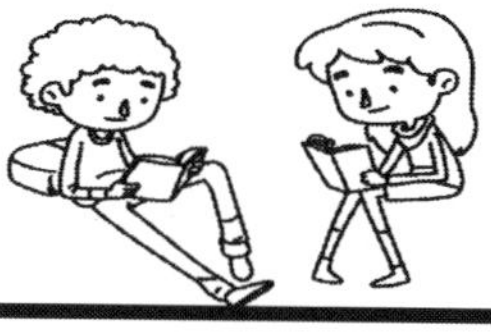

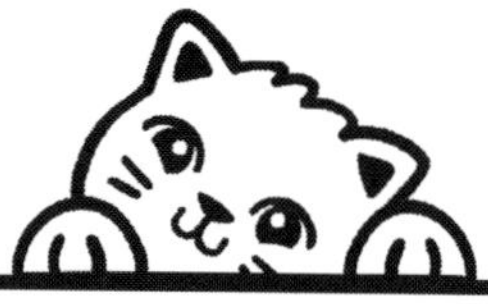

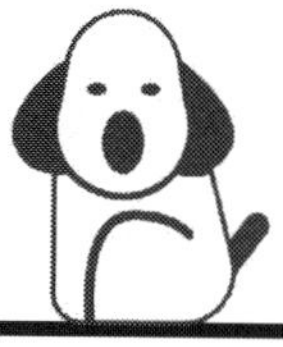

Write

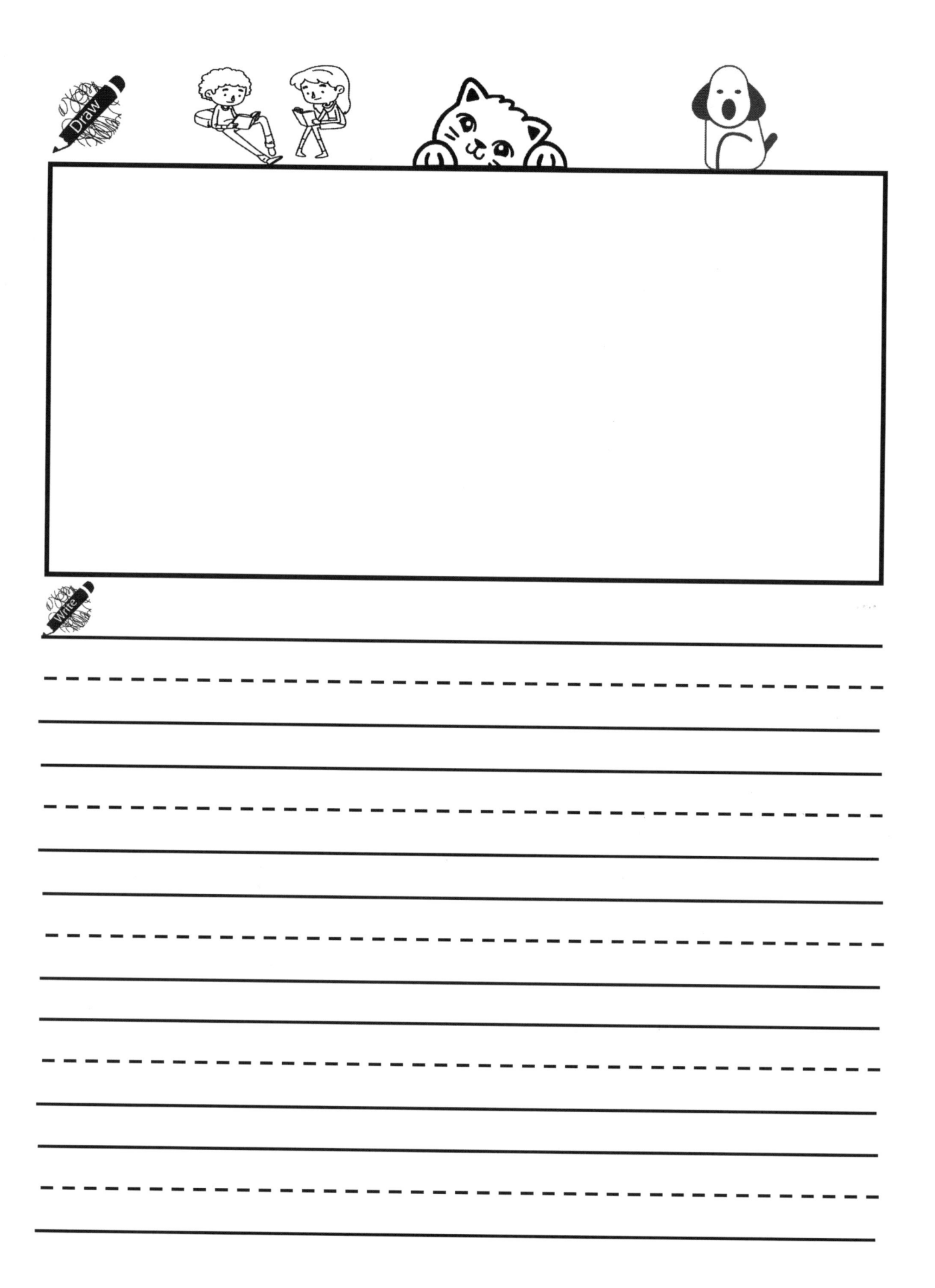

Draw

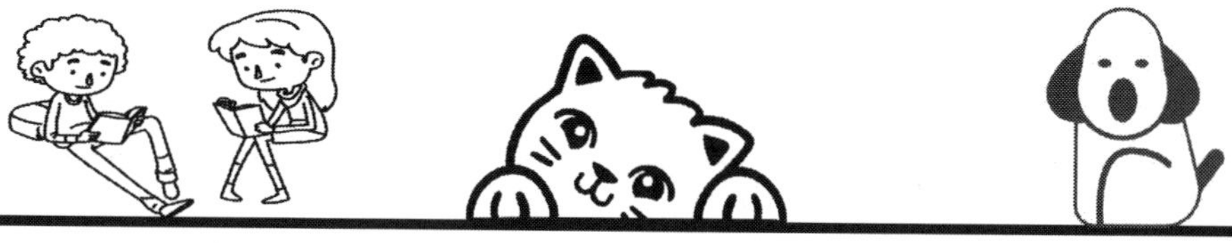

Write

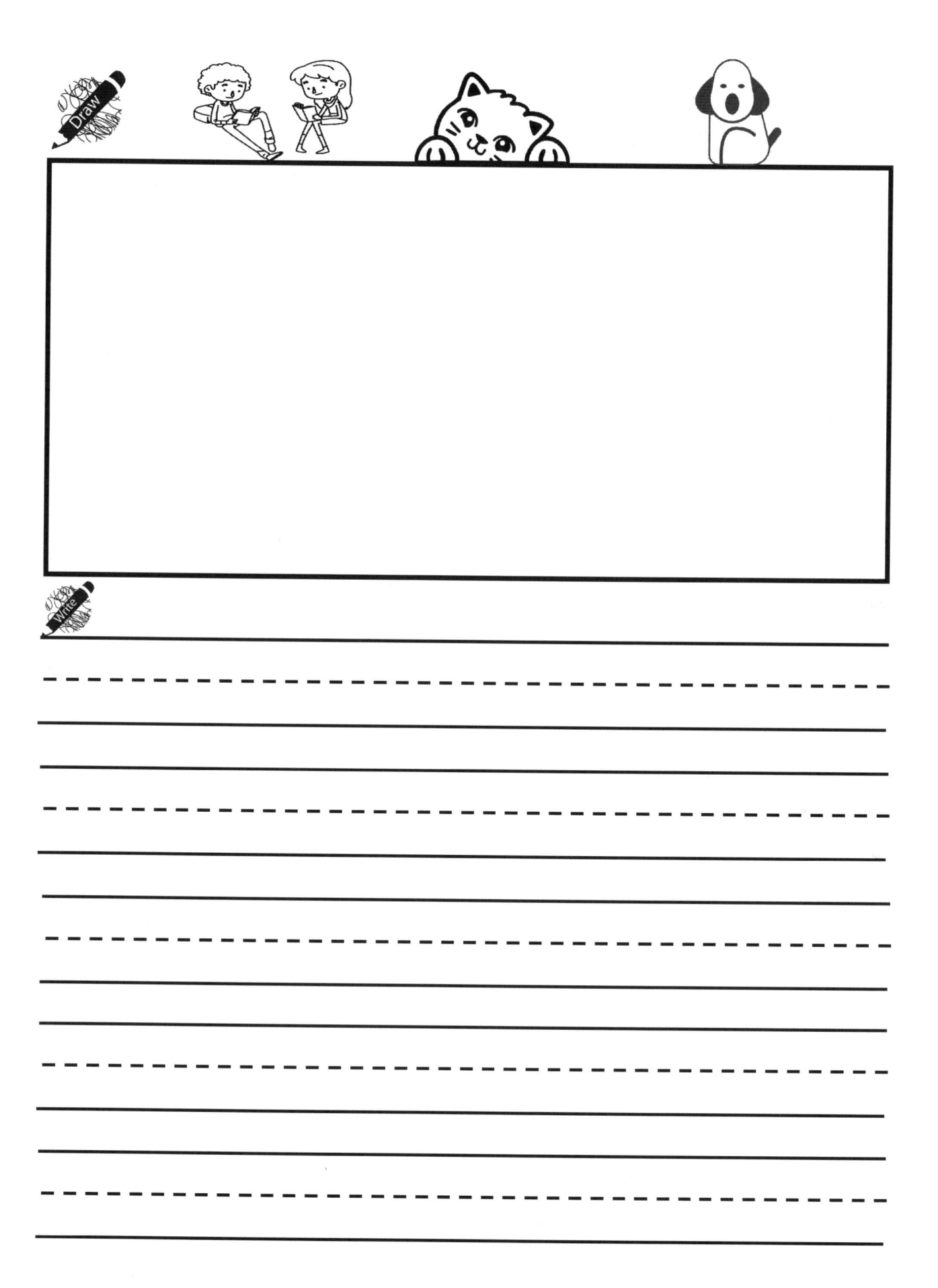

Draw

Write

Draw

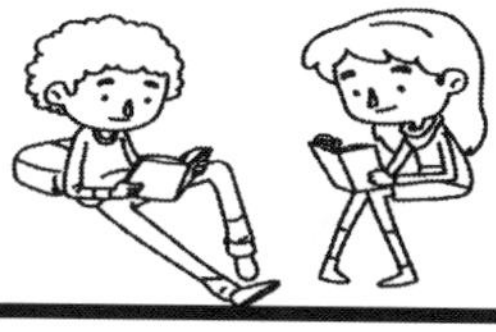

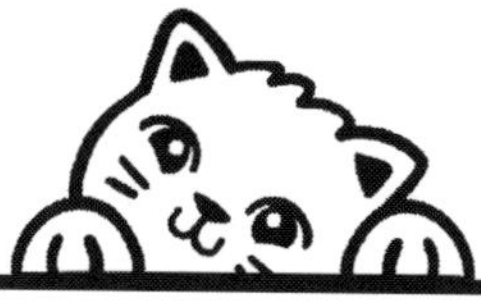

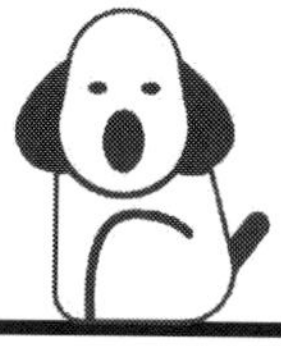

Write

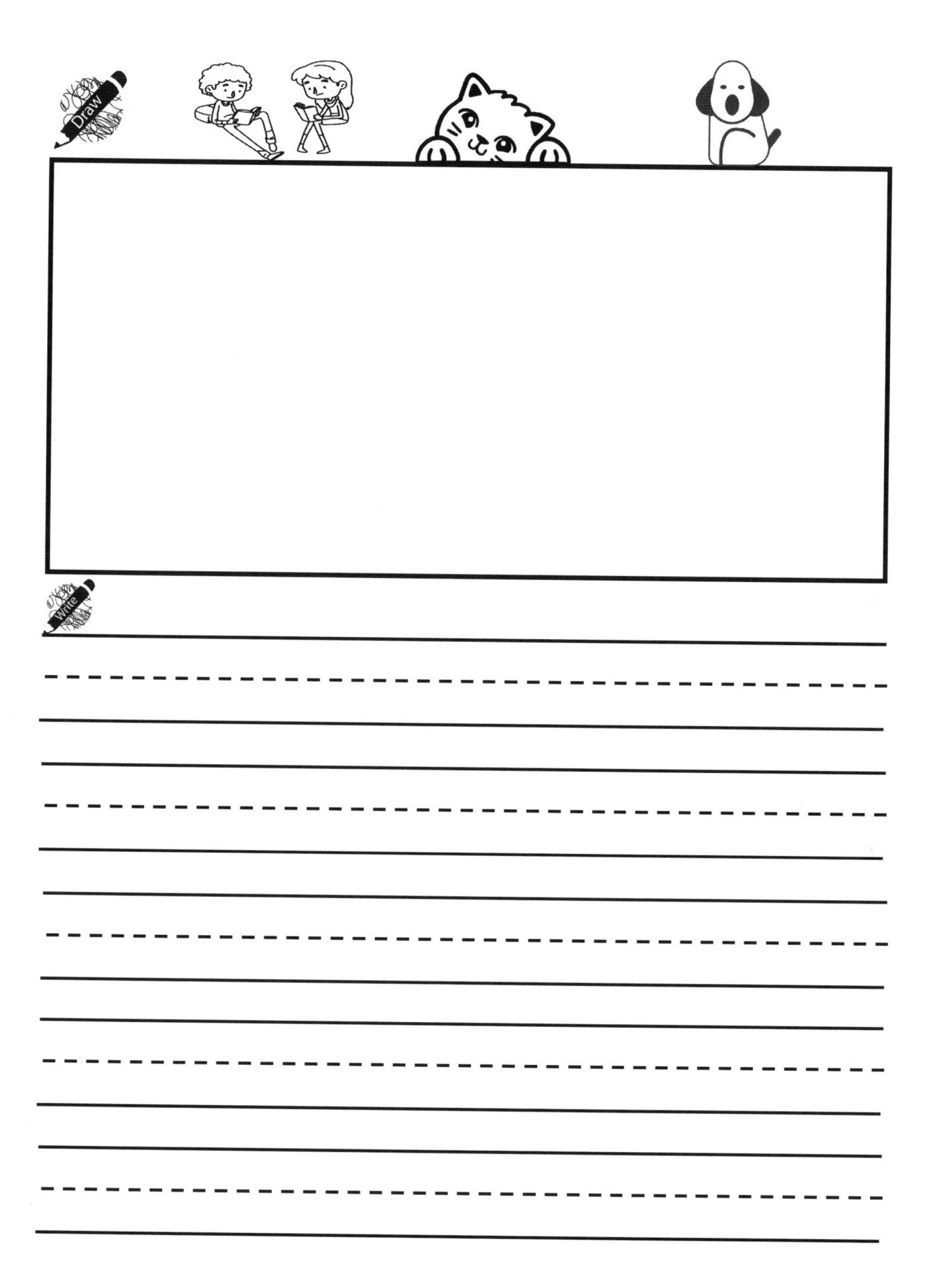

Draw

Write

Draw

Write

Draw

Write

Draw

Write

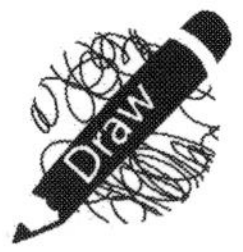
Draw
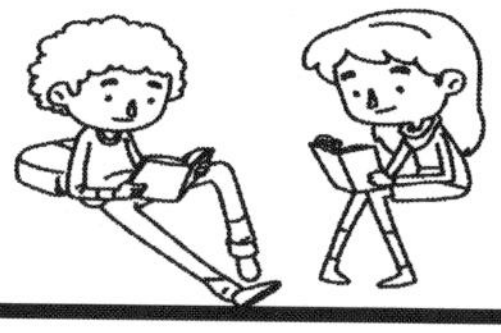
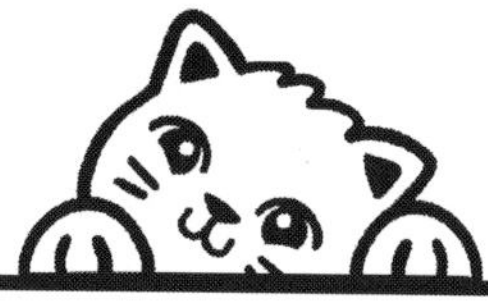
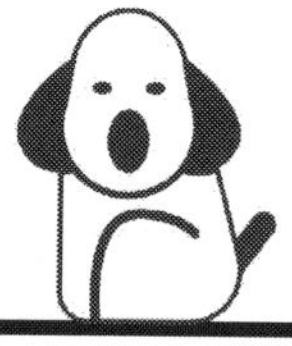
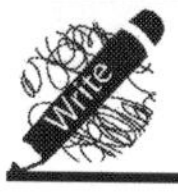
Write

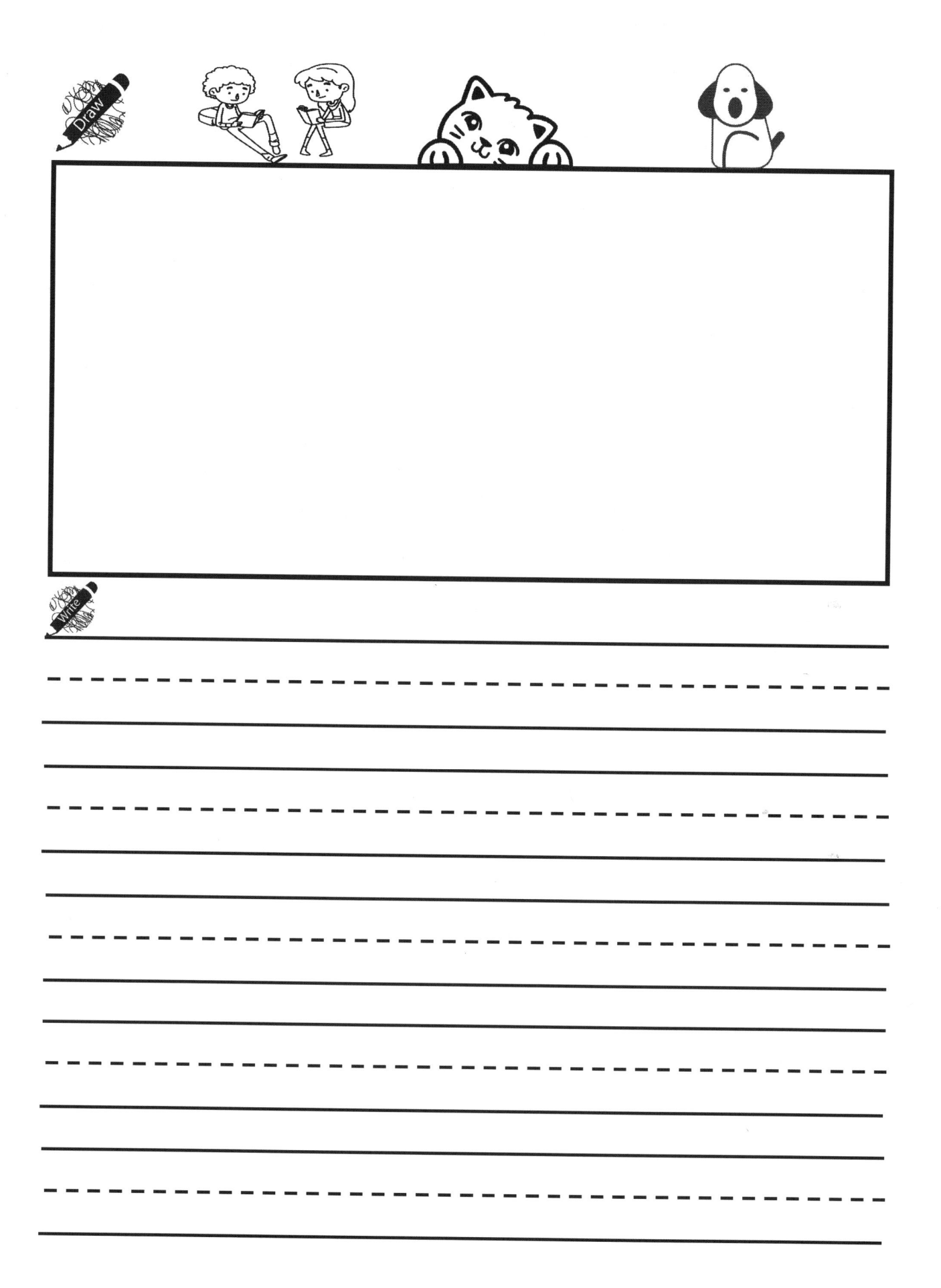

Draw

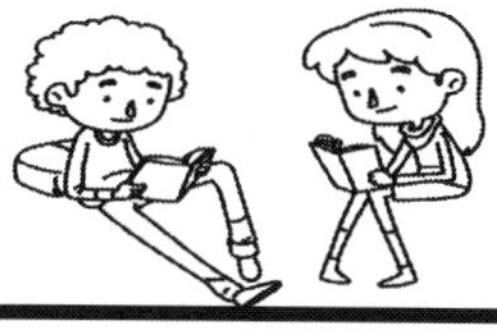

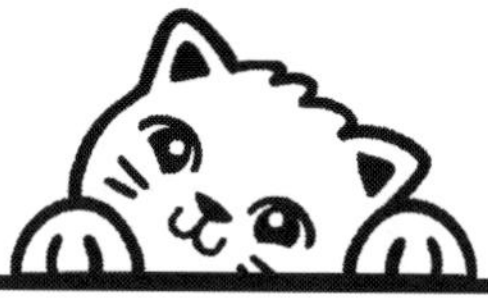

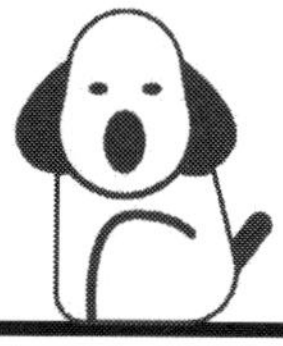

Write

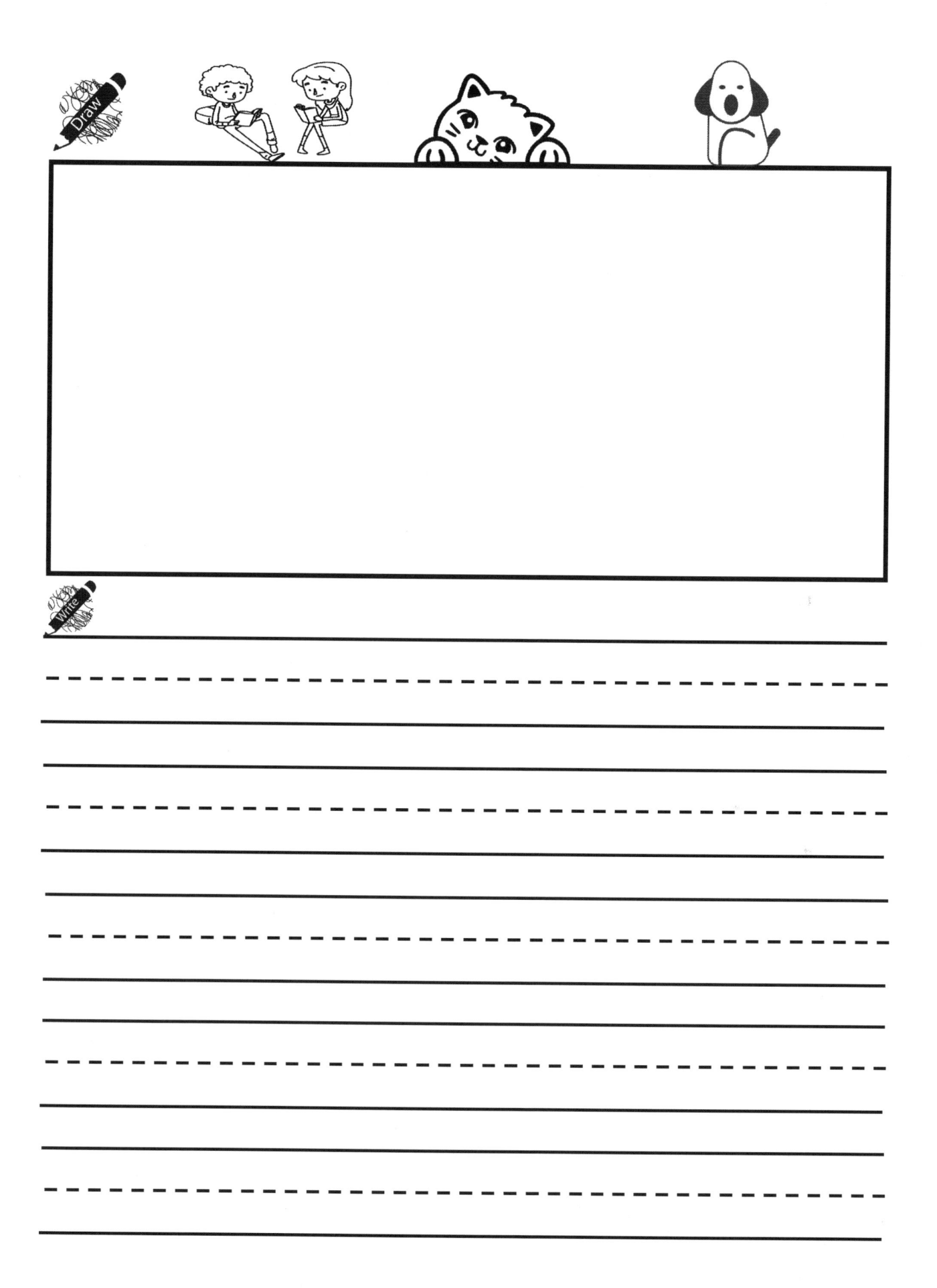

Draw

Write

Draw

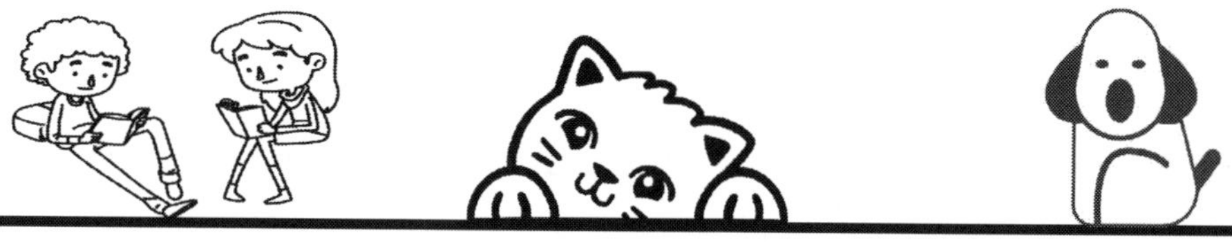

Write

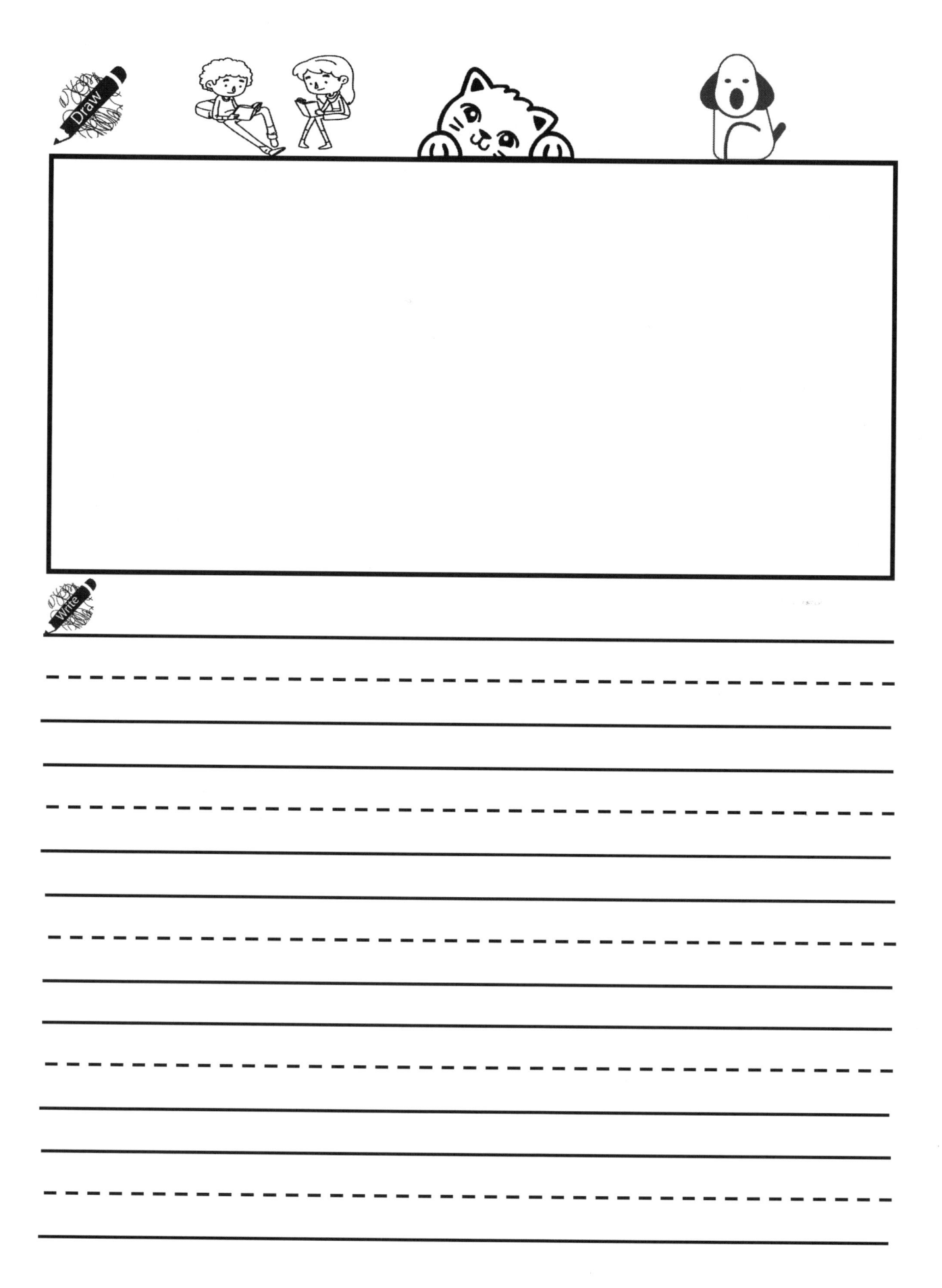

Draw

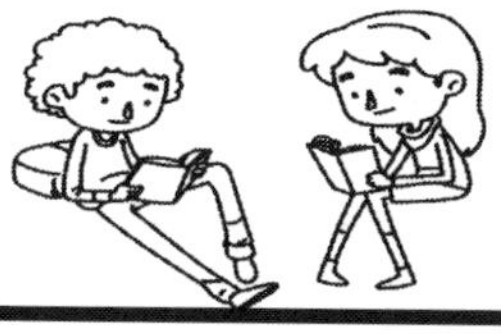

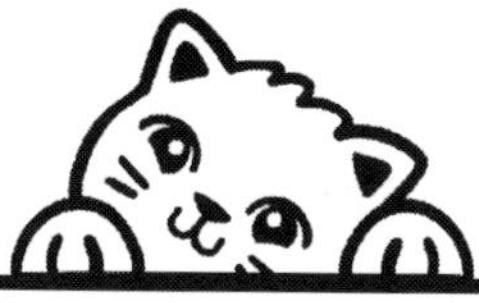

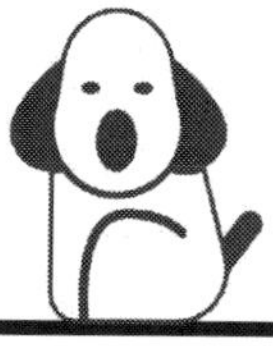

Write

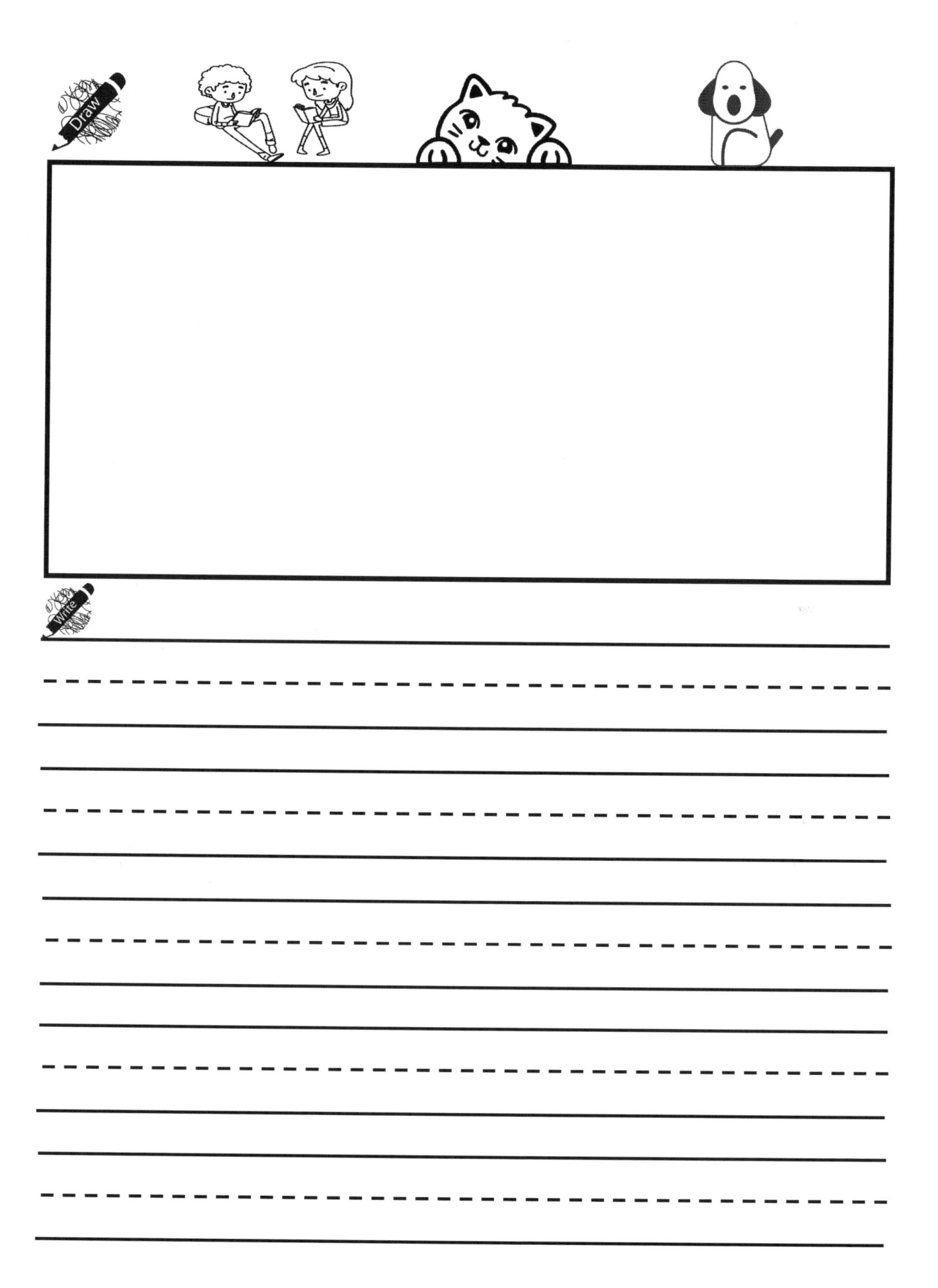

Draw

Write

Draw

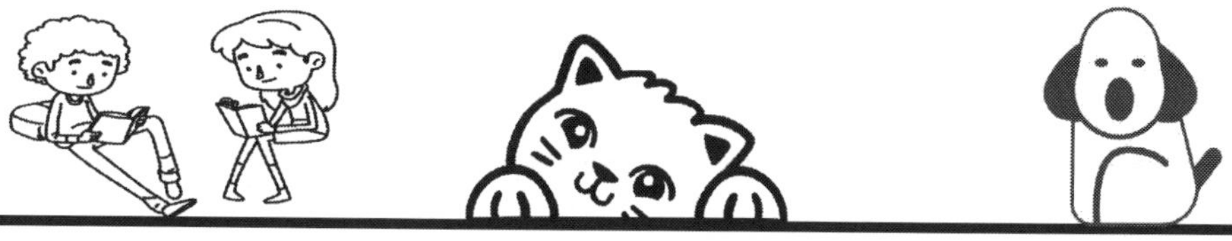

Write

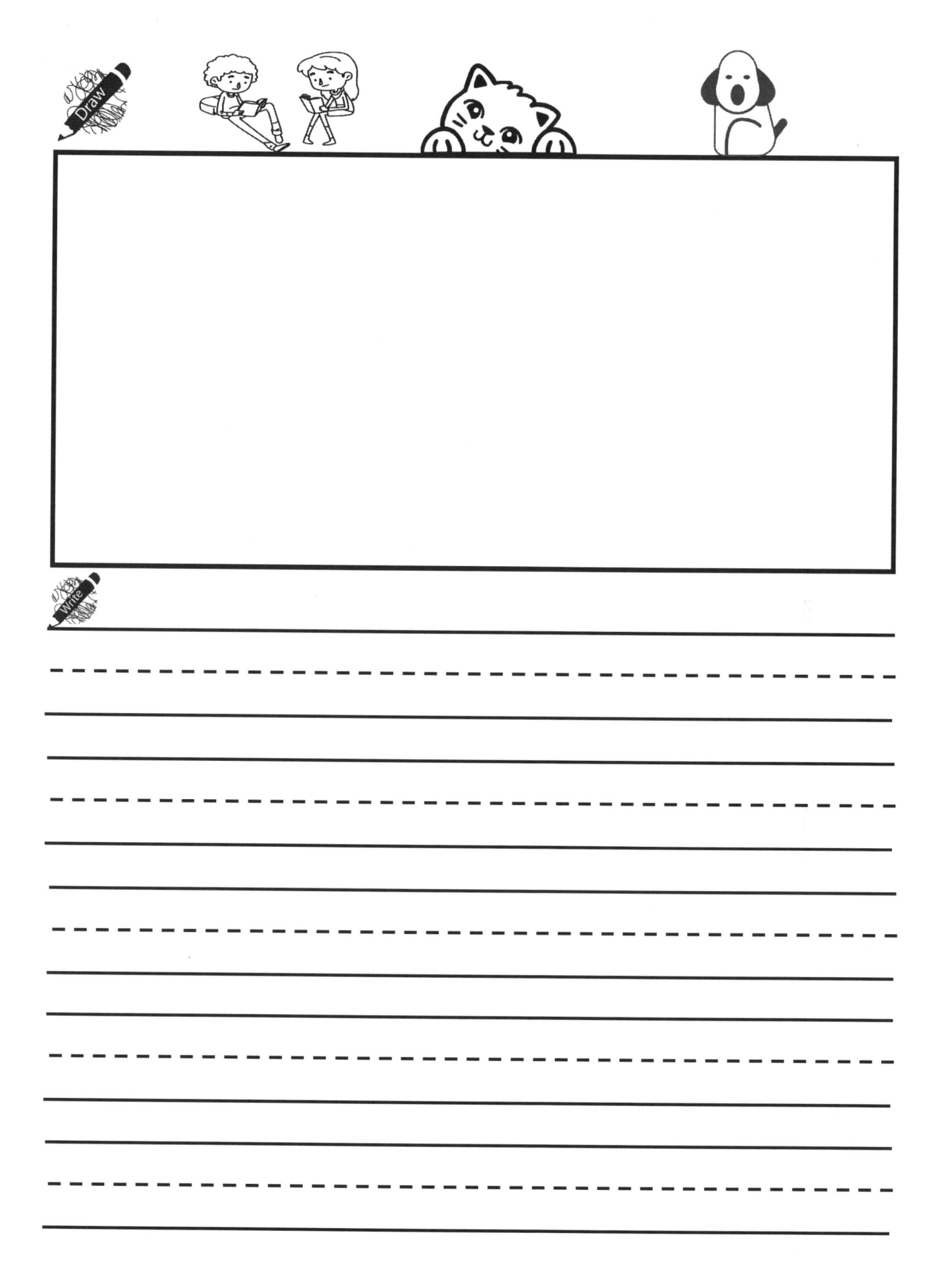

Draw

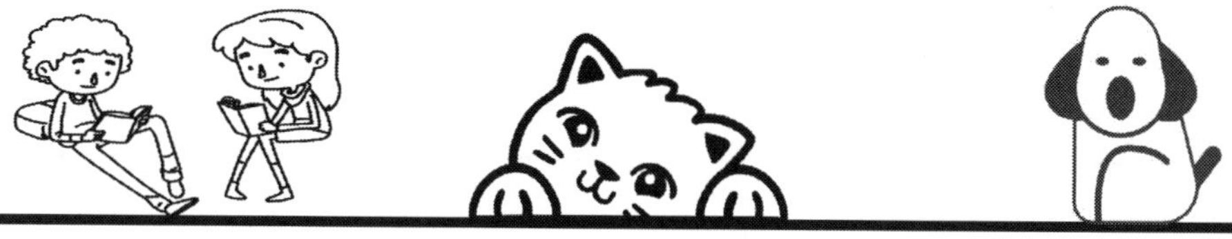

Write

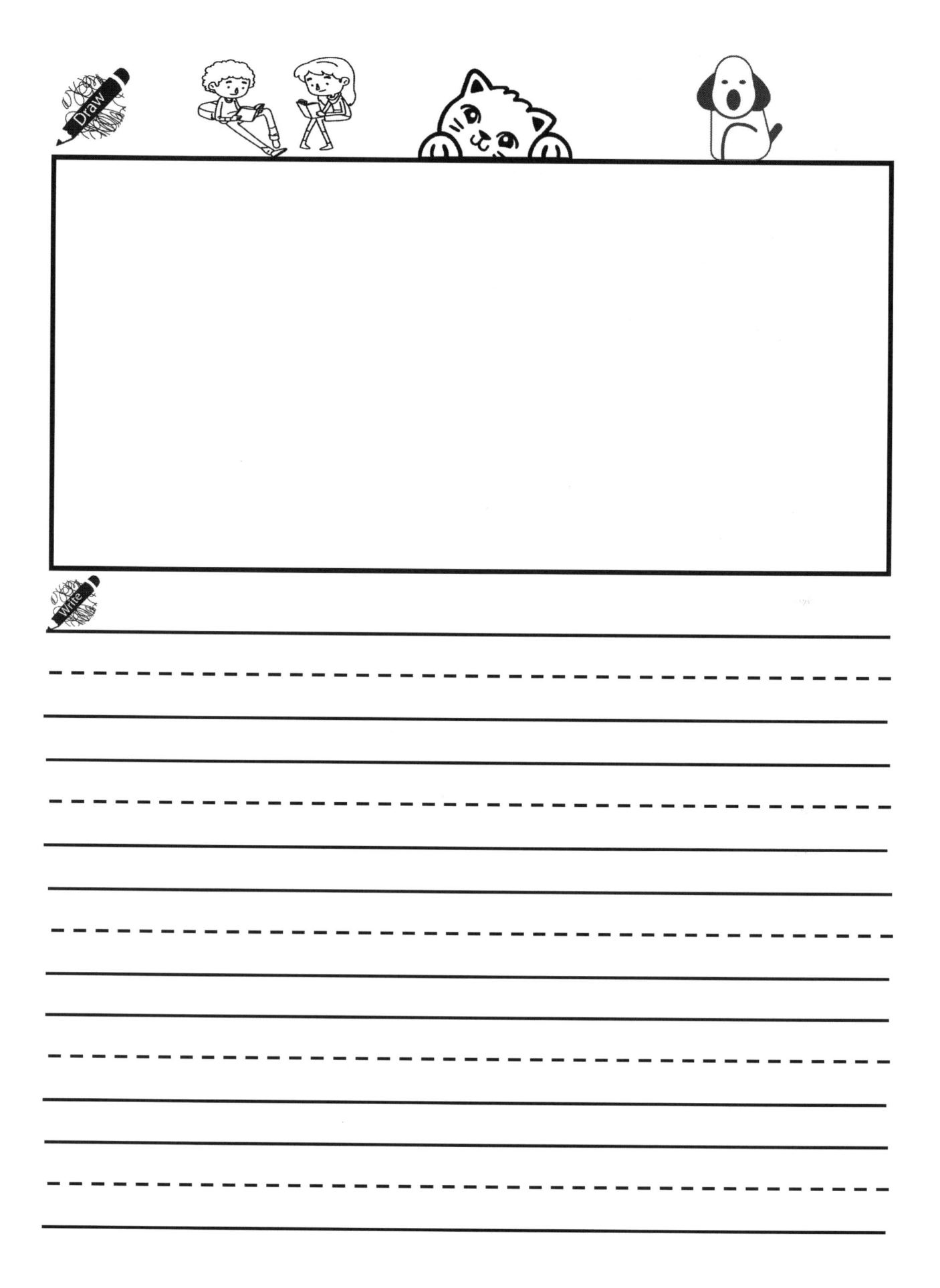

Made in the USA
Columbia, SC
27 September 2022